RISE ABOVE

Rise Above

Interventions in Business and Social Impact

Emmanuel Nyame

**RISE ABOVE WAS LAUNCHED AT THE UNITED
NATIONS HEADQUARTERS, NEW YORK, U.S.A.
DURING THE HIGH-LEVEL POLITICAL FORUM ON
SUSTAINABLE DEVELOPMENT.**

JULY 16-17, 2018

RISE ABOVE

Copyright © 2018 Emmanuel Nyame

All rights reserved.

ISBN-13: 978-1722699888
ISBN-10: 1722699884

ALL NET PROCEEDS FROM SALE OF THIS BOOK WILL BE DONATED TO EDUCATIONAL COMMUNITIES WORLDWIDE, INC. TO HELP BRIDGE SKILLS GAPS IN GHANA.

DONATE | START A FUNDRAISER | GET INVOLVED
EDUCATIONAL COMMUNITIES WORLDWIDE, INC
WWW.EDUCOM.WORLD

All rights reserved. No part of this publication may be reproduced, distributed, or transmitted in any form or by any means, including photocopying, recording, or other electronic or mechanical methods, or by any information storage and retrieval system without the prior written permission of the publisher, except in the case of very brief quotations embodied in critical reviews and other non-commercial uses permitted by copyright law.

For permission requests, please contact **The Publisher** or "The Copyright Permissions Coordinator" at: eknyame@gmail.com
Printed in the U.S.A.

First Edition 2018

Professional Editing By Nathan Gadugah, Bernice Garr, and Susan E. Sackey.

Cover Design by – Enoch Hagan and Solomon Danquah
Cover Photography by - Lambert Worlanyo
Cover Photo Stylists - Hamid Vijay and Neal Dodoo

Praise for RISE ABOVE

"You can always get a dish, sometimes even the ingredients, but how often do you get the recipe? Emmanuel gives us all of that in *Rise Above*. He gifts us his formula for success and shares the tools that took him years to refine. It is one thing to acquire knowledge and skills for the self but another entirely to take the extensive time it takes to translate it for others. Thank you for sharing your personal journey, your pain, and mostly your triumphs. This will be used and valuable in helping others to transform their own lives."

- **Leila Steinberg. Founder, AIM4TheHeART; Former Manager & Mentor, Tupac Shakur.**

"Emmanuel is a passionate, committed entrepreneur who truly wants to make a difference, and improve lives of those around him. He is hard working and focused, and I can't wait to see the many great things his future holds."

- **Jeff Hoffman. Entrepreneur (Priceline.com, uBid.com), Proven CEO, Worldwide Motivational Speaker, Board Advisor, Film & Music Producer.**

"Emmanuel is a dedicated and focused advocate of African entrepreneurship. He has spent much of his young life bridging local initiatives with global enablers. He is a creative problem solver who understands the broader vision. He brings world-class professionalism to the serious work at hand, and we're all better for it."

- **Kwame Dougan. Attorney, Scotch & Palm.**

"In *Rise Above*, Emmanuel gives young people everywhere further inspiration to fight off societal pressures to conform and instead create value and impact for society. Opportunities are everywhere for young people, and Emmanuel - using vulnerable and powerful stories of his life experiences - provides a roadmap to capture them. Amazing!"

- **Justin Lafazan. Co-Founder, Next Gen Summit; Author, What Wakes You Up?**

"Emmanuel Nyame is an inspiration to his peers. He has worked tirelessly to support young entrepreneurs get access to the capacity building, coaching and financial resources they need to start and grow their own businesses. His sheer passion and commitment in supporting young people has served as a catalyst and encouragement for organizations and private individuals to donate their time and money to help Emmanuel succeed with his youth empowerment entrepreneurship initiatives."

- **Aba Quainoo. Executive Director, MEL Consulting Limited.**

"Emmanuel K. Nyame has written a must-read primer for anyone interested in youth empowerment and sustainability... Read this book - and learn from one of the best youngest minds I'm proud to know and collaborate with."

- **MacJordan Degadjor. Co-Founder, SocialGood Ghana.**

"The world needs more bright, passionate and dedicated young leaders like Emmanuel. As a former economic officer for the U.S. Embassy in Ghana, I have had the privilege of seeing first-hand Emmanuel's work unleashing the God-given potential of youths across Sub-Saharan Africa. Emmanuel's personal story overcoming adversity to become a leader in youth entrepreneurship is an inspiration for a new generation of aspiring young achievers across the continent."

- **Thomas Chen. Former Economic Officer, US Embassy Ghana.**

"Mine has been a life changing experience and I really wish to let the world know that no matter what you want or who you are, you can make a bold statement with your life, your decisions, and your story.

This statement by Emmanuel Nyame encapsulates the

essence of his book *Rise Above*. In this book, Emmanuel speaks about his journey so far and details events in this journey which have led him to where he is now. He outlines the enduring lessons he has learned, recalling the number of times he failed but through persistence got back on his feet. He recounts starting his business as a young entrepreneur and the challenges he faced, which informed his passion as a mentor for startups. What stands out from Emmanuel's story is his ability to draw a lesson from every experience and incident that has occurred in his life; life lessons that we can all learn from. Notable among these is how his involvement with Junior Achievement set the tone for his entrepreneurial journey.

Told with a simple, accessible narrative, Emmanuel's story will resonate with everyone. The book achieves its aim of encouraging, motivating and challenging readers to rise above the challenges of life, pick lessons from failure and forge ahead with great determination."

- Elizabeth Bintliff. CEO, Junior Achievement Africa.

About RISE ABOVE

No force of nature can break your will to self-motivate. There's one direction and the reverse. The series of resilient moments that follow take this same line: constantly restoring self-belief as though there is no dearth. Every attempted buildup will slip and fail between his impulses. Every process reclaimed except the attainment of his goals - to be his truest self.

Young people have the potential to transform our communities, with their capabilities becoming more vibrant and impactful each year. Organizations worldwide are exploring how the youth can be a pillar to reduce setbacks in education access, create jobs, and quickly improve the societies where they belong.

How can this transformative approach get into the hands of local stakeholders and changemakers worldwide? Emmanuel narrates his journey to self-awareness and provides guidelines for anyone who wants to be successful with their talents, passions and entrepreneurial skills.

DEDICATION

To God be the Glory.

I wish to thank the Almighty God, my family and all my dear siblings, who have in one way or another aided me to be who I am today.

To my business partners and associates, I cannot thank you enough for your consistent motivation to achieve higher laurels.

I thank God for the amazing women of substance, my mother and all the other women who nurtured, sacrificed, supported, inspired and trusted me. To Aunty Grace of Amerol Nursery School, Miss Dora Dankwa, Mrs. Beatrice Odonkor, Ms. Aba Quainoo of MEL Consulting, Mrs. Kristen Bergman, Mrs. Adriana Resendez-Casso, Sara V. Stealy, Mrs. Chrysula Winegar, Anne Rosenthal, I say thank you.

To my alma mater, Accra Academy, that is where this dream started. I really cannot say much but to the relentless teachers who believed in me, I say "Thank You" for the great works that you do. Keep it up!

CONTENTS

Acknowledgements

Foreword

1	Introduction	
2	Upbringing	4
3	Friendships	13
4	Rise Above	15
5	Myths	27
6	Start Small	35
7	Responsibility	39
8	Winning Team	42
9	Productivity	47
10	Interpersonal Relationships	51
11	Goal Setting Mechanism	58
12	Moral Integrity	68
13	Job Creation	73
14	New Year Deception	76
15	Become a "Usain Bolt" Start Up	81
16	You May Fail And So What?	85

17	Make Sound Financial Decisions	89
18	Be Skillful At What You Do	96
19	Visualising	102
20	Impact Story	111
21	References	123
23	About The Author	125
24	Your Free Gift	126

ACKNOWLEDGMENTS

This book consists of my experiences in business and career. I have carefully compiled all the good, the bad and the ugly moments which have catapulted me to the level I am today.

I am not there yet, but I can boldly say that my experiences gave me great leverage over many challenges I faced in life, both big and small. These experiences, I hope will also consistently keep you motivated in order to achieve your goals and objectives in life.

Huge thanks to all who played a significant role in this this project-editors, photographers, researchers, associates, and friends. Frankly, your thoughtfulness and never give up attitude have added tremendous value to bringing this book to the world.

Exceptional thanks to my advisors, mentors, the church and dedicated supporters for the constant teachings and moral values they imparted to my life. We are all not perfect, but our walk with our maker makes us capable of staying true to ourselves.

Finally, to these amazing people who are dear to me, I just cannot thank you enough: Mr. Baba Adongo, Patience Afful, Adu Serwaa Sandra, Ms. Senam Aseye, Mr. Mac-Jordan Degadjor, Mr. Lawrence Fianko, Mrs. Bridget Yaya Simpi, Samuel Seffah-Nyame and Mr. Benjamin Djartey.

FOREWORD

Congratulations! In your hands is a potentially life changing book.

Rise Above shares stories of possibility, hope, and how to live your life to its fullest potential, regardless of your current situation.

Are you ready to start something of your own? Inside of you are the seeds of greatness. It is the young people who represent the promise for a better future around the world. Entrepreneurship will offer you an opportunity to explore your unlimited potential to create your own career path, while showcasing what is possible for others to emulate.

Having worked with over 100,000 entrepreneurs in over 60 countries, I am blessed to be working with some outstanding people on a shared mission to ignite the human potential of aspiring young entrepreneurs.

Emmanuel Nyame is one of these extraordinary people. Emmanuel embodies a spirit that says, " We can do better by taking on some of the biggest challenges we face in the world, inspiring others along the way." Ghana StartUp Cup and Africa StartUp Cup Business Acceleration Programs are two excellent examples of his commitment and determination to empower the youth of Africa. He focuses on individuals taking ownership of their lives with self-determination, moving past the chains of dependence on someone else determining their future.

We can all learn from Emmanuel's entrepreneurial journey. He has moved past the adversity that comes with growing a business and personal brand in Africa. These transformational experiences have molded him into a source of great inspiration. He is self-made, afraid of

nothing, and is willing to step into the great unknown to see his vision become reality.

Now more than ever we are in need of young dreamers to take action. I've worked with people from all corners of the world and from many backgrounds and education levels. I've learned that anything is possible as long as you are willing to believe in yourself and work hard enough to turn your dreams into reality.

Embracing and applying the lessons found in Rise Above is an excellent step towards making your dreams come true.

Sean Griffin

Business & Life Coach

Founder, StartUp Cup & GriffinWorx

Washington D.C.

RISE ABOVE

1 INTRODUCTION

This book, Rise Above, is my first published book and it is my heart. Since you are going to be better acquainted with me after reading, permit me to call you friend. The moments spent putting the pages of this book together are very precious to me. It represents many years of change and though I know it is not truly complete, I wrote this book with you in mind, being careful to include the nitty-gritties of my experiences and lessons. I am eager to share them with you!

This book goes beyond motivation. I am of the view that each individual on earth needs to make a conscious effort to bring to life that which they desire. There are so many things to be thankful for in my life. I have been privileged to enjoy one of the best years in my young life - of course not on a silver platter but simply put, it has been full of hard work and nothing more than consistent attempts at achieving excellence.

The images on the cover of this book are a deliberate

attempt to reflect how I have transformed into the person I am today. The first image looking to the side represents the many things I have witnessed in the world; the disappointments, struggles, and the challenges that I encountered. Having picked up a great deal of knowledge in the process, it transformed me into an individual who is now focused and determined to make a difference in society, which is represented by the second image looking straight ahead, at you!

Rise Above, provides in-depth knowledge about how my life began, the ups and downs, including my early years in school, church and business. It touches on pure life exposure and the lessons learnt which I believe can be a guide to all who wish to have personal growth and development in any chosen career path. I implore you to grasp the lessons here like you would a shield, for they will surely be of great service to you in the battles of life!

Early Years

"The number one way that we can address these long-term challenges of poverty, of education, is to invest in early childhood education." Julian Castro

Let me ask you this, friend. Would you be pleased to go through the same kind of education you were given, if you had the chance to relive your childhood? I expect the answers to this question to differ from one person to the other. What is vital is that you may have an entirely different answer after you have completed this book. A simple paraphrase of the quote above is that; as a society or nation it is very necessary to prioritize the education of our youth. They are the world's future leaders. I often hear the saying that children are the future but it became one of those clichés I took for granted until I became a testimony of what education can do to a young child. In the coming pages I will highlight the importance of educating a child from my perspective.

Education, an amazing ladder to greater opportunities

Whoever invented formal education did us good! Formal education has exposed me to a number of opportunities I never thought I would have in my young life. You must note that, although formal education is a blessing, it is one thing going to school and another thing having the discipline to excel against all odds to become relevant in society. I settled for the latter. That is the ultimate goal. However, I found out that most students get derailed from their vision due to negative influence from friends, close relatives and others who do not have the boldness to achieve their dreams. This book therefore gives solid counsel on the various ways you can take advantage of the opportunities that formal education presents, to make you a better person.

Lessons from what I call 'my learning experiences'

The US president Theodore Roosevelt was right, when he said nothing worth achieving comes easily. I want to stress that I may not be there yet, but my struggles and pain gave me reason to do more in order to become a better person each day. When I was a child, I used to hear so many stories about life in the boarding school. Some of the stories sounded a bit weird while others were nothing but scary experiences. Among those which gave me chills and left me wide eyed was how the seniors were ruthless in punishing their juniors at school. I dreaded the day it will be my turn as a junior, but somehow I found solace in the thought that it was only going to be for a while. Then came the moment when it was my turn to live the experience. I entered the boarding school at Accra Academy hoping with time, things had changed but it was a mere deception to the self. The horrifying stories became a reality. They were the same as the ones I heard or maybe worse! However, just as every cloud has a silver lining, each story, for those who lived it, came with a wealth of experience. As you progress through the pages, you will discover lessons from the numerous learning experiences that life handed to me. These lessons changed my life for good. I desire to let the world know that no matter what you want or who you are, you can make a bold statement with your life, your decisions, and your story. Here is my story. May the pages that follow inspire you to chase your dreams.

2 UPBRINGING

"Train up a child in the way he should go, And when he is old, he will not depart from it." Proverbs 22:6

You will agree with me that school is fun to be in especially when you are young, innocent and you really have nothing to do, no major responsibilities and nothing critical to think about. Aunty Grace, the Headmistress had unique ways of making us feel at home, even though some tutors demanded a lot from us. This is how my day always seemed at Amerol Nursery School. To be honest, I was always eager to learn something new and to become a person of substance even at that tender age. I really did not know exactly what I wanted but the thought of becoming a solution to the many problems in my country always kept pushing me to become better. As a young boy, I was very enthusiastic about aeroplanes. Anytime I saw one, it was a jaw- dropping moment for me. It was as if I had just witnessed the second coming of Christ! I was not matured in my thinking at the time and thus it always provided the slightest opportunity for me to rethink my choice of future career. At first I wanted to become a pilot, then a doctor and then an engineer. Come on, I wanted to carry the entire world one day!

Nursery school days have usually been the start of life for most people. For me, it gave me a good start. I would begin the day by going to school with tears trickling down my face just because I will miss my mum and dad. I had to be lured and persuaded with toys and sweets just to agree to go to school each and every day. This made my going to school less traumatic. Parents sometimes have unbearable tasks – it is all about patience and sincere love. Have you ever wondered how you managed to learn all there is to learn about writing alphabets and getting conversant with strange symbols at a tender age? If you're reading this, well done, you overcame that challenge! In school, I was not sociable and was more introverted, preferring to be quiet and to stay out of trouble. In many ways I am still very introverted and I believe my quiet nature enables me to ponder more about life, be highly observant and successfully make plans for the future. Going to school was also helpful, since I had the chance to meet various people from diverse backgrounds. Thankfully, in Ghana where I was brought up, the standard of nursery schools has not lapsed but has rather improved. It is a very good starting point for most people.

****

Everything was quite different this particular morning. We all did not expect this to happen and we had no choice in the matter either. I had little experience with this although I always saw my mum do it at home and church. It was prayer time that morning! All the students, me included, were assembled to sit on the floor in front of the school and we were asked to pray. My little self may have wondered, "Pray?? How is that done?" To my relief, the woman leading the prayer asked us to recite the prayers after her. This was the first day I actually learnt how to pray which led me to believe in God and in myself. I accept that the kind of training I received in nursery school was not just formal education but it also included training to gain self-confidence, a necessary ingredient for success in life. Many people go through the challenges of life not knowing what to do or who to talk to. Some face deep-seated problems that may at worst, cause them to resort to suicide as a solution. Whereas it has become very necessary to find quick solutions to our problems, I believe that the act of prayer and meditation are helpful tools which could be used as means to effectively connect with one's inner being, the soul. For me, during these "quiet moments of reflection" I try to be thankful for all the things that are in my life. I also speak to a trusted person, usually my parents or a church elder about my problems in order to find a lasting solution and also to maintain my sanity. In your bid to chase your dreams, problems will be encountered. During such times many may try to further discourage you by making you believe your dreams were absurd in the first place. I've been there before! Don't pay attention to them! They may advise you to cut corners and settle for second best, something lower than what you desire to achieve, but it is important to believe in yourself and to be mentally focused. The exposure and training I received as a young child, starting from the home and in early childhood development at school, helped me to believe in myself such that I gained confidence in my future. Staying focused in life is critical because no matter how bad things may turn out, it cannot rain forever. Surely, the best is yet to come.

The Road Not Taken

I am inspired by the works of Robert Frost in his poem The Road Not Taken. I have a feeling that this poem has a lot to teach young people coming out of school and colleges on how to live their lives and I would like to quote it here:

Two roads diverged in a yellow wood
And sorry I could not travel both
And be one traveller, long I stood
And looked down one as far as I could
To where it bent in the undergrowth

Then took the other as just as fair,
And having perhaps the better claim,
Because it was grassy and wanted wear;
Though as for that the passing there
Had worn them really about the same,

And both that morning equally lay
In leaves no step had trodden black.
Oh, I kept the first for another day!
Yet knowing how way leads on to way,
I doubted if I should ever come back.

I shall be telling this with a sigh
Somewhere ages and ages hence:
Two roads diverged in a wood, and I--
I took the one less travelled by,
And that has made all the difference.

I find this poem very inspiring because it addresses the dilemma we sometimes face in making decisions, concerning the paths that we should take in order to attain our goals. In choosing which path to take, we tend to be greatly influenced by both positive and negative external and internal factors. We should be aware of what we allow to influence our decisions. We may not know the end result of our choices but what we can do is to take a bold step after carefully considering our available options.

A closer look at the first paragraph of Robert Frost's poem talks about two roads and how it is impossible for the persona to travel on both, at the same time. He is faced with the dilemma of whether to follow the path less travelled or the path which is common to all. Whichever decision he takes is going to alter the direction his life would take. Thus, the first thing he does is to carefully study the two roads. As you read further, you will find that the persona realizes both roads will involve parallel experiences. Moreover, the journey through both paths seems to be prosperous. The persona has to choose one and based on his observations he chooses the one that he prefers most, with a step of faith. He is displeased that he has to sacrifice one road for the other. The persona does not say whether he is satisfied with his choice or not. The most important statement he makes is that his choice will make the difference in how his life will turn out in the end. Though he cannot help but ponder over the possibilities he could have achieved if he had taken the first road, he consoles himself with the idea that he has chosen a unique road, that which is less travelled.

What does this teach us? An inevitable aspect of life is making choices. The choices we make determine how our lives will eventually become. In making choices, we first need to understand who we are, what we want, and how we want our lives to turn out.

Such bold choices, as that of the persona in the poem are what we need to make if we want to achieve our dreams. I will add that you must consider carefully what options are available and make sure that you understand what each option entails. This is beneficial in starting any kind of endeavor, so that the chances of you making the best or most suitable decision will be higher. I must admit, I wasn't able to do this in the early stages of my life. As I grew, I began to gain knowledge about how to make the right choices. Now this is what I want to emphasize. Often, you do not have to see the whole picture before you take a bold step. It is important to just man up! What do you seek? You have brooded enough over the options! Take the bull by the horn and go for that one thing you desire. In life, there are so many people who are basically lost because they cannot determine what they really want. Most of the time our hearts know what we want! We only refuse to obey because we think our dreams are not good enough, we do not have the right resources or that our dreams do not conform to the status quo. Also, because of lack of confidence and fear of the unknown, we tend to sit on the fence and remain stuck where we are. Sometimes we think it may take too long to achieve our dreams and it's going to be a lot of hard work. These are mere excuses! We then go ahead to admire the efforts that others are making to achieve their dreams and we are tempted to copy them, thereby neglecting our own dreams. If this applies to you then it's no accident that you're reading this. This is your wake- up call. Determine your dreams and go after them.

Many young people fall prey to peer pressure and may lose the way. Wonderful ideas and dreams have been abandoned because others chose a line of ridicule and discouragement. Other times, because no one else was willing to support that remarkable discovery we lost hope, did not pursue it and rather followed the crowd. Such negative external factors among others should not be considered in making your choices. Surprisingly, some parents also fall under the umbrella of negative external factors! Yes, parents must guide their children in making decisions, especially career choices, but they are not to make it for them. Worse still, they should not force their children into a career path they are not interested in.

Follow your instincts and do the unimaginable! Dear

friend, this is the kind of mentality that will help you achieve your dreams. So many people in the world are doing things simply because they see other people doing it! You must stay true to yourself. I want to inspire you today. I was always afraid of starting something new in the past. My reason was that I feared it will fail. When I began to think out the project, I often only saw problems and not the opportunities and as a result I lost my focus. This sapped my energy to be creative and prevented me from tapping into available resources which would have easily brought the project to life. Unfortunately, the projects died and were blown away with the wind of fear! In the process of making choices, you must never succumb to the voice of fear, an internal factor that stifles dreams.

As a young person, it was a big challenge for me trying to focus on what will be successful. I spent time rather imagining my failures. I had an extraordinary fear of failure at the nursery level, though I believed in myself. The difficulty was in how to shut out that fear when it came knocking. Fortunately, I was a very good student. I always topped the class and won many awards. I was so intelligent that I was skipped two classes ahead of my mates. This was a great achievement and my parents and siblings were extremely proud of me. I learned to become a deep thinker at an early age and this helped me greatly. I remember at some point in my life, I was able to achieve certain difficult tasks by relying solely on my tutors but soon enough, I became independent and was able to achieve a lot. This I did by connecting deeply with my soul, my vision and intuition, to know what I truly desired and to guide me every step of the way. This has become the secret of my success.

The CEO of Virgin Group Richard Branson made a powerful statement in one of his books which still resonates with me. He wrote, "The brave may not live forever but the cautious do not live at all". This is a profound life changing statement which should make any progress-minded person daring enough to take difficult decisions in life no matter the odds!

So, on this particular sunny afternoon at about 2 p.m., quite fed up with the whole routine, I decided to take a bold step. I was only five years old. School was about to close and while I sat waiting for my parents to come pick me up, I told myself that there was surely much more I could achieve. I decided not to wait any longer. Seeing that the security guard was nowhere to be found, I took my bag and started walking out of the school. I can recall feeling thrilled that I was finally embarking on an adventure.

At that moment, I wanted to do something I had never done before. It was like taking the road less travelled and challenging the status quo. There was no need to wait to be picked up by my parents. I believed I could venture out on my own. I walked quite a long distance away from the school until I saw my elder sister approaching. She shouted, "Where do you think you are going?" I replied that I wanted to make it home on my own! She looked at me, smiled and walked with me home, probably assuming it was just a childish hyperactive urge. The message I am trying to send across is that you should not follow the crowd. You have to take the road less travelled especially when your dreams call for it! Do not wait for things to happen. If you have a dream, you need to work towards achieving it now. If I was able to fearlessly walk out of school that day at the age of five years, without waiting for anybody to instruct me, then nothing is ever impossible for you to achieve once you put your mind to it.

SUMMARY:

a) Dream big
b) The importance of providing children with a good educational foundation
c) Believe in God and in yourself
d) Maintain your focus in the face of adversity
e) Know what you want and let nothing stop you from achieving it
f) Beware of the fear of failure that causes you to lose focus and tricks you into believing that another's dream is more achievable than yours.
g) Learn to make use of your intuition and vision
h) Be daring, take risks
i) Make bold decisions after carefully considering all options
j) Stay true to yourself

3 FRIENDSHIPS

"Life doesn't make any sense without interdependence. We need each other, and the sooner we learn that, the better for us all."- Erik Erikson

Day by day I became accustomed to my environment. I was always of the view that no matter the situation that was presented, there was a way out. Church was beneficial in diverse ways. I became very committed to church service on Sunday mornings. I will wake up as early as 5 a.m. to iron my clothes in order to be on time to church. Aunty Kar had taught us to buy a small notebook for Sunday school lessons. I did not like the idea initially but I had to obey because I did not want to displease the Sunday school teacher. She also taught us about accepting Jesus Christ as our Lord and personal Saviour. These moments were special to not only me but the other Sunday school children.

At that time, I was very timid and quiet, always waiting for others to make the first attempt to speak to me. Our teacher would always point a finger at me to answer questions. I guess that was her way of helping me overcome my shyness. I devised a strategy that anytime I attended church I would sit next to someone I did not know. I did this throughout all the three stages of Sunday school and somehow I became popular. Everybody was so interested in getting to know more about me because I always sounded different. One had to study the bible to prove oneself worthy of graduating from the Sunday school. It was quite tough yet I gradually picked up on lessons every Sunday. Our main task was to memorize as many verses in the Bible as we could. Through this task, bonds of friendship were established. All of us became very close. Sunday school eventually came to an end and we had to begin a new journey in the youth church.

Today, the friends I made in church and in school are the ones I always fall on whenever I need help. Imagine that I had not taken that bold step to find a way out of my shy character to make new friends every single time I attended church. I cannot imagine what would have happened along my life's journey. Friendship gives us the opportunity to understand people and appreciate life from different perspectives. Whenever you make a new friend you learn something new. I remember when I needed legal advice but I didn't quite have the huge sums of money quoted by the lawyers. It was my friend, Gabriel, whom I fell on. We met during Sunday school. Friendships can never be underestimated and never look down on anyone. The person you look down on today can certainly be your savior tomorrow. Build friendships but invest in quality friendships. I am saying all of this to reinforce the necessity of having good friends.

SUMMARY:

a) For every challenge, there is a way out.
b) Build friendships, they will be helpful in your journey.
c) Never look down on anyone.

4 RISE ABOVE

"Obstacles don't have to stop you. If you run into a wall, don't turn around and give up. Figure out how to climb it, go through it, or work around it."- Michael Jordan

The sound of a bell reverberated over and over again, followed immediately by a loud shout from the bell boy, "break over please!" This was the first sound which welcomed me to the school. It was my first day at Primary One. I took the chance to get to know all new students so I could make new friends. One good friend I made in nursery school was Gilbert Addison but unfortunately, I couldn't find him among the new comers. I faced my first day boldly as I felt lucky to have been admitted to start primary one.

Whenever school closes, I arrive home to a happy family excited to have me back. Every morning my mum packed snacks for me so I never went hungry at school. Such is a mother's love. School was pretty interesting even though it was a new environment for me. I loved school and like every serious student I always did my best to be regular.

Dad never allowed me the peace at home and always drummed the need to study hard. I did. It was a struggle in the beginning but I had to endure. Through it all, one question kept popping up in my mind - what do you want to become in the future? In fact, our teacher, Miss Ofori asked the same question and she wanted nothing but precise answers. The responses were all too familiar- a doctor, a lawyer, a pilot and many of those childhood fantasy jobs. Even at that age I wanted to be so many things- a doctor, a pilot or an engineer. Not convinced with the answers we gave, Miss Ofori asked us to go and read about the various professions and come the following morning with a more definite answer and what to do to become who we wanted to be. That was when I discovered what was actually required to become all of the above. At home, I had an insightful discussion with my parents. My father took me through what each career option entailed - excessive commitment to mathematics, if I really wanted to become what I was dreaming about. Was I capable of doing anything mathematics, let alone be a champion at it? I kept asking myself.

I started being realistic about what I wanted to become because none of the things I heard sounded good to me. I was consistently impressed with the way our tutor encouraged us to accept and work hard towards what we wanted to become. I began to take math seriously. This was class one and because of that single most important question, the consciousness of what to become in future had become increasingly manifest. This was not an easy task for young children.

On and on my life in school became an interesting journey until the use of cane by our teachers buried the passion I had for school. My grades began to fall. Out of 25 students in class I placed an uncomfortable 23rd position. What was the problem? Had I not completed all my homework and assignments? Or was it a mistake from the calculations? Did I slack, thinking everything was an easy road for me? Or had I met tough students who were more ambitious than me? Too many questions came to mind which I had to answer before I got home to break the news to mum and dad. I was afraid my mother may get angry and not cook my favorite food. In fact this was my first experience where I actually learnt that nothing in life comes easy. Clearly, you have to always fight for what you want in life because nobody will ever do that for you. It is always important to remember that no matter how good you are, there's someone who knows more than you do. Nevertheless you must rise above such challenges. Never allow a setback to determine your next move. Simply rise above it and you'll definitely have reasons to move forward. Years passed by and my academic performance kept deteriorating. I seriously did my best every single day just to improve my grades but all efforts proved futile. To be honest my parents were unhappy and they always had a problem with my performance. When it was time to collect our report cards I will always be faced with the fear of not performing to the best of my ability. By and by this became a part of me. Although I had improved as an average student I wasn't as good as I wished to be.

Gradually, I moved on to the 5th grade. At this point it was as though my mum was fed up. It was not the best of situations. I was active in class discussions but not on the paper. I wondered if it was fear of examinations that created this roadblock for me. I did not seem to understand what was going on as things became difficult by the day. Anytime I told my friends about it they thought it was a lie. According to them I was one of the brightest people in school. Was I really the smartest? Or was it that I was not being truthful to myself? It so happened that my mum surprised me in school one early morning. She came to speak to my teacher about my abysmal performance in school. I was shocked she would do that. My teacher then walked both of us to the headmaster upon my mother's request. It was a very emotional experience. My headmaster was my biggest fan - but for him to hear that my mum was not pleased with my academic performance, got him worried. He asked me a question which I will always remember. "How would you feel if you became the President of Ghana?" I was surprised. "I would feel so good about myself for such an achievement," I answered quickly. Then he advised that I should translate that emotional feeling to my academic work because that passion and drive can help propel me to the academic heights I dreamt of. With a little hesitation, I nodded in agreement. I just did not want things to escalate and turn into something that I wasn't prepared for.

From that day onwards, my teacher hurled one question after another at me during classes. I couldn't afford to go to class without preparing. Little by little, I finally made a position among the top 10 in class but it wasn't enough for me. I could do better. Funny enough, I began to feel that everything looked staged. As though I was only acting in a manner to prove myself worthy. Is school not supposed to be a place to learn new things and open up a person's thinking abilities? Or was it only a place to prepare children for exams? Sadly in the early 2000's, studying and passing an exam appeared to be the only objective I had in school. I got somewhat confused but with time, school became an interesting place to be and I did my best, abiding to rules and regulations. The early morning 'mental'- a quick question and answer session on basic mathematics- in class stimulated me enormously. During the mental session, the only way to escape the fury of the teacher was to answer his questions correctly. The more wrong answers recorded, the greater the number of lashes he served but there was an even greater terror which each one of us endured back at school and it got worse any time the academic year was drawing to a close. The thought of being repeated in the same class was a huge psychological trauma for me. The terror was twice as much when it was time to be promoted to the Junior High School level from the 6th grade. Depression set in and I would always curse myself because of the school system that got me frustrated every day. My performance in the 6th grade was nothing to write home about and on the final day of school that year, just before we received our reports I got really scared because I knew deep within me that things had not gone well. However when I opened my report card, it was boldly written: "You have been promoted to Junior High School!" I had a huge sense of relief!

In Junior High School (JHS) we had to study new subjects in addition to the ones I struggled with back in the 6th grade - Agriculture Science, Catering, Technical Drawing, among others. Meeting new friends who had been transferred into my school from other schools, and hearing stories from their end made me feel better since I realized compared to others, my problems were not that great as I thought.

My story at the Junior High level was markedly different from that of the 1st to 6th grade which we called primary school. My academic performance became optimum and I became the reference point for most teachers. Every teacher liked me because I was studious and I motivated others to become better. Helping the teachers mark the papers of our junior students made me toast of many teachers and the envy of students. My JHS experience was nothing short of awesome until that day when the mock exams results were released just before we sat for the Basic Education Certificate Examinations (BECE). The BECE is what determines if students can continue education at the Senior High School (SHS) level. Results for the mock examinations were out and I had 5% in Mathematics! I became the laughing stock of the class. It seemed as if everybody was happy that I got that score. I remember clearly the kind of depression that I went through. Just when I thought that everything was going on well with my academics, I fell back. I cried that day not because of my score but because I studied a lot to merit a much better performance. The questions were generally difficult because it was an attempt by the teachers to prepare us adequately for the final BECE exams.

After this failure I became very close to my math's teacher, Mr. Onyi. He started advising me about life and the various things one must do in order to be successful. We became very good friends. Mr. Onyi always caused a stir in class with his wisdom and principles. He would always give the class reasons why we needed to work hard. One thing I recall him saying was that not everyone in the class would be able to enter the university. He asserted that others may end up unsuccessful, whilst others may live a wayward life. He will always conclude by saying: 'But it all depends on your determination and commitment to make a difference in life.' That statement resonated with me and has since been one of my secret armors for success in life.

In order to perform well in the next mathematics mock examinations, I decided to secure a home tutor. We would meet in his house right after school and study from 5pm till 10 pm each day. It was stressful but in the end I needed to make it in the exams and also surprise Mr. Onyi. Little did I know that my effort to go the extra mile was the basic principle for success! The extra mile is a lonely path only few are willing to take. I did what others were not willing to do and prepared feverishly every single day. I began to understand certain mathematics principles and it also increased my level of confidence in the subject.

I wrote the second mock examination with so much

confidence and I topped the class. The extra mile is a place of sacrifice and devotion to the things that are important. In life, trouble usually beats us from left to right and leaves us worrying all the time. Nevertheless, I am of the view that the same challenges we face also direct us to take the right steps that will help us overcome. I decided to transfer that same seriousness to my other subjects. I began to stay late in class after school to study and I also signed up for extra classes in other schools. I learnt from other students who were knowledgeable in the various subjects. I was hard on myself and always took the opportunity to be better in all the subjects. During those times, internet access on mobile phones was not available. High costs and slow internet connection at internet cafes made it quite difficult to learn online except to check emails which were usually filled with junk and spam mails. All the same, I pulled through.

It was time for BECE and I wrote the paper to the best of my ability. Our headmaster promised to organize a party for all graduates after the examinations but it never happened. After the examinations, we converged in the school to pray. It was the final day in school and we swapped gentle hugs with tears of joy. Mobile phones were not so common at the time so the best we could do was to either give our email addresses or give our parent's telephone numbers to our friends before parting ways. Five months later, the BECE results were out and I excelled in all subjects. Mr. Onyi called me to his class and told all the students to emulate my lifestyle and be serious about making a change in their lives. I was so happy to excel in the exams, but to be called in front of students and to be used as a symbol of motivation was a badge of honour I wore with pride. I left Junior High School with one thing in mind - in life, nobody knows tomorrow. Therefore never let the fear of failure prevent you from working on your ideals and goals in life.

Accra Academy was my first choice Senior High School and I got admitted to study Business. Accra Academy is well known for business and with business as my preferred subject, I could not have chosen any other school. I did not have much interest in Science. Due to my growing interest in mathematics in JHS I was compelled to read business in SHS. Moreover, I really had interests in investments and entrepreneurship. First year in school was awesome. Meeting different people from different walks of life was refreshing. I spent time hearing and learning from other people's experiences.

Soon the academic year was almost over with exams fast approaching, as well as the yearly awards ceremony organized on the last day for the best students in each class. I was so much into this whole idea of making new friends that I paid little attention to my books and voila! Although my results were good, it was not enough to grab an award at the Speech and Prize Giving Day! Somehow, I was a little surprised to learn that the student who sat next to me was awarded for excellence in the examination. He was such that he would only talk to me during his leisure time and would go back to study. Through this I learnt: "It is all about you". Sometimes you need to live life for yourself and make decisions that would propel you to a different stage which can help you achieve your goals and dreams in life. In short, do not say yes to someone when it means a no to you.

I went all out in my studies and began to apply those principles I used when I failed my 'mock' mathematics in JHS. I became friends with my books. As a matter of fact I would study day and night until I was fully satisfied. I also started learning ahead of the class so I would be able to understand each topic even before the teacher came to class to teach. It really paid off and in my second year at school, I topped the class. Everybody was amazed. In all three terms I topped. On one of those occasions, one of our Elective Mathematics teachers called me to stand before the class after distributing the marked scripts. He said, "You see this gentleman, you all have to emulate him". At that moment I was confused and humbled at the same time, not knowing what the reason for the commendation was. It turned out I had scored 99%, the highest any student had scored in two decades of his 20-years teaching career, according to my teacher! I couldn't stop myself from beaming.

My glory days were not over. One fine morning our Economics teacher Mr. Asun walked into the class and informed us that the school had received a letter from the Government, the Ministry of Finance to be precise, inviting Accra Academy to compete in the Annual Quiz on Finance and Economic Planning. He asked the class to select three students who could better represent the school. My name came up. Indeed I felt special at the moment but I was very scared of facing the cameras at a quiz which would be televised. I tried my best to understand the responsibilities that came with accepting such an invitation before going ahead to accept it. We were ten students in total and our teachers trained us for several weeks ahead of the quiz competition. The goal was to train all ten highly rated students so that at the end of the training the school can select the two best performing students to represent and a third person as backup. I got selected! Whoop! Together with Robert Adjei we were selected to represent Accra Academy against fifty schools nationwide. Mawutor Isaac (May His Gentle Soul Rest In Peace) also got selected as the backup. It was tough but I truly believed in the training that our teachers had provided. Prior to the quiz competition, our Headmaster, Mr. Samuel Ofori Adjei, called us into his office and with a word of motivation he told us to make Accra Academy proud. "What you do with this competition could determine what you will become in future," he told us.

On the first day of the quiz, we had to battle five schools for the Greater Accra regionals. We managed to answer all questions. It entailed five rounds in all, and we were leading by the end of the third round. We thought we had won until another school led the scores at the end of the fourth round by a stretch of twenty five scores. Pressure started mounting and the proud Accra Academy became the laughing stock of the audience. I did not give up. My partner kept saying, "Let's see how it goes". I told myself we were winning this competition! I could see our teacher in the audience signaling me to calm down. That was exactly what I needed. The last round was about mathematical calculations. This was my strength. This section of the quiz allowed the fastest student to answer each question for five points. There were six questions in all, which meant that in order to win the competition we had to answer all questions. We answered everything amazingly well! We won by a difference five marks to progress to the next stage of the competition. It's important that when faced with adversity, we must not be quick to throw in the towel. We moved on to next stage of the competition, and won again.

My most memorable experience was during the Semi-finals of the competition when every school had heard that we were a threat. This time around the tide began to turn. We were last from round one until round four. At this point all hope was lost. Truthfully I did not know what had come over us. "How would my friends feel when they see this on TV?" I said to myself. It was the final round and as usual we had to answer Mathematics questions real quick. Once again, magic happened but we did not win. There was a tie between us and another school. We both had to answer the next question correctly to determine who would win. The question was asked and both schools began to work out the answer feverishly. Just when I was about to answer the question, a lady representing the other school pressed the bell to answer and I gave up instantly. In my mind, we had lost and I did not know how we were going to explain this to our Headmaster and teachers who were hoping for nothing less than a victory. However a miracle happened and we did not lose. Yes! The lady who had pressed the bell to answer the question got it wrong and we were supposed to give an answer. At that moment I felt relieved. My muscles became very relaxed and I was ready to answer to the question. I pressed my bell, answered correctly and surely, we won.

Moving on to the finals of the whole competition was a dream come true but then it meant that we had to prepare very well if we wanted to grab the ultimate prize. To be honest the finals was smooth. It looked like everyone was afraid of us now. We nailed it! And we won! Out of fifty schools nationwide, my colleague and I were able to lead the school to victory. As part of prizes for this competition, we won some cash for ourselves and for the school which was later used to improve the business department. I gave thanks at church. At this time of my life, things were really going on well for me. I became the Vice President for the youth section of my church and I was proud of myself. One thing I learnt from this competition is that in life, challenges come our way to test our strength. No matter what happens to you, keep moving forward towards your goal. Never stop to please anybody or mourn the temporary defeats you may suffer in life. Rather, try to focus on the good aspects and become the best that you can be. Nothing is impossible.

SUMMARY:

a) Take advantage of opportunities to network.
b) It's important that children know what they want to be in future, early in their education so they can start working towards it.
c) Nothing in life comes easy, you must fight for what you want.
d) While chasing your dreams, don't allow setbacks to determine your next move.
e) Rise above every challenge. Don't give up on your goals because of temporary failures.
f) No matter how bad you think your situation maybe, there's someone whose situation is worse.
g) Never lose your hope, things eventually get better.
h) Always be willing to go the extra mile in your efforts to succeed.

5 MYTHS

"It's a lack of clarity that creates chaos and frustration. Those emotions are poison to any living goal." – Steve Maraboli, Life, The Truth and Being Free

My life as a business person stood out while in secondary school. The opportunity came on the wheels of the Junior Achievement company program. Richmond Anku and Lawrence Omane, my dormitory mates approached me to discuss the opportunity of having me join this program during one evening studies. The Junior Achievement company program allows students to start companies and sell the company's products directly to their fellow students. We were given a manual on how to build a team and other necessary steps needed to kick-start a student run company. Initially, I was not convinced but because I had just read the book, Rich Dad, Poor Dad by Robert Kiyosaki, I had a strong urge to become my own boss and impact people rather than seeking for jobs after school. I accepted the offer and we started to think about ideas that we could sell. I subsequently contested for the position of president of the new company but I lost brutally. I later reapplied to serve as the VP of Productions and won.

During the initial stages of the company we encountered a lot of myths and did not know how to go about certain ideologies and assumptions. Throughout my entrepreneurial journey, I have come across very intelligent young people who are itching to start their own businesses. I believe it is great to have a dream and it is okay to want to own a business empire or a group of companies. However, there are certain myths that either prevent us from executing our ideas or even progressing to the next stage when we are hit with challenges, be it financial or other problems. Is it easy to start a business anyway? Before I became a part of the Junior Achievement company, this, among others was the thought I had to contend with. I am hoping that these suggestions from my personal experience can clear your doubts and point out why you may be unable to sign that contract, increase revenue, or take your idea to the market place. What kind of business would you want to start?

Let us first clear some myths:

Capital

One common myth that most young people face is that one needs huge capital or equity investment to start a business. Many startup founders go through the hustle of creating huge budgets for their businesses for their first six months of operation. We started the Apex Junior Achievement Company with just GHs 20 (US$5). We were able to manage. Instead of going to borrow monies to start, all 5 founders donated towards the initial capital. Then after making our final decision to sell bags and souvenirs for students, we entered into a trade agreement with producers of these bags which allowed us to pay them when we had sold each bag! It was that easy. We made a lot of money. No matter how brilliant your business idea might be, no one would have 100% confidence in investing in it unless you are able to prove your go-to-market strategies, revenue generation models, demonstrate that your assumptions have been tested and finally a unique selling proposition has been developed.

We later decided to float shares to the student body. Students really purchased with passion due to our new service - the student loan service. We offered to provide loans to students who were 'broke' and needed funds to go home when school was on vacation. We capitalized on an opportunity which many students were witnesses to. Most students had to stay on campus close to a week after vacation just to find monies to transport themselves back home. Our intervention was to help them by providing soft loans to transport them home. We made a lot of profit which our shareholders really enjoyed. Instead of asking yourself how much capital you need for your startup, it is essential to find out how little you will require. Usually when your budget shows huge sums as your capital requirement, you get discouraged along the way because it will look so impossible to acquire such huge amounts. However, when you break your costs down, you realize that things become easier and starting out would be convenient for you.

Business Plan vs. Business Model

What is the difference and how is this causing chaos? A business plan is a formal statement of a set of business goals, why they are attainable and the steps for reaching those goals. It may also contain background information about the organization or team members attempting to reach those goals.

A business model is however an action plan that outlines how the business will actually operate. It also identifies the sources of revenue, the intended customer base, products and details of financing. It is usually a one page document and it's as brief and precise as possible. You really do not need a business plan when you are starting your business. Such plans usually take so long a time to write due the detailed research needed. You may also need to do a comparative market analysis, talk to people in your industry and start giving data about your expected revenue stream. This process is usually daunting. You do not have customers yet how do you determine your revenue stream? I believe business plans are for existing companies that have a past or some track record of operations so they can use it to forecast the future! I recommend one develops a business model, go to the market quickly to test the assumptions. A business plan would only get you day-dreaming! The project we started at Accra Academy never had a business plan. We only had to submit annual reports to Junior Achievement when we were done with everything.

Team Work

Often, you hear in the news and on the front page of magazines that successful CEOs have expanded their businesses or have been praised for achieving a milestone in their respective businesses. Nobody succeeds alone! You may have the best business model but you certainly cannot do everything yourself. It is essential that each startup forms a team of three

– The one who brings the Idea, a Marketer, and a finance expert. The one who introduces the idea is usually referred to as the Founder or co-founder. The Marketer, otherwise known as the business developer, provides the clear marketing plan or strategy to attract customers and eventually, profit for your business. The finance expert is usually a person with enough knowledge in fund raising and managing the finances of the company. Each team member works hand in hand with others to achieve the company's set goals and objectives. So if you see in the magazines or in the news, the CEO of a company being praised for his good work, remember – He's representing His Team!

Start Big

This is one common myth encountered by most people. When you look at huge companies like Microsoft, Apple and the rest, we often think we also need to start that way. We begin to budget for a big office space, vehicles for business, several office staff etc. However the good news is that many successful companies look huge now, but they started small and gradually grew to the conglomerates we see today. You do not need all these inputs to start operations. Endeavour to start as small as you can. There are always certain ways of running your business without having to rent a large office or buy vehicles. For instance you can operate from a home office in the initial stages. There are always many innovative avenues of doing more than enough with little resources. In recent times, innovation hubs have sprung up across the world and are doing amazing stuff. You can actually acquire an office space for as little as $5 (per day) and you get access to free internet, a conference facility, a desk and a table. This is a really low cost for someone desirous of starting a business. It is necessary to start small, and remain focused on your business concepts and ideas. All the very successful companies in the world had to start from somewhere in their little closet. Most entrepreneurs also start from home (in their garage, etc.). Think about starting big and you will only place a stumbling block in between your dreams and your actions. We started our company without an office and only had $5 in our bank account then.

Profits

The most common reason for starting a business is to make profit and it is very critical too. However that should not be your number one goal. When you focus excessively on making profits, you may get discouraged along the way. There would be times when you would incur some losses and this might discourage you. Due to increasing costs of doing business and unfavorable economic conditions, normally meeting set objectives and targets is impossible in the short term. This is why you should not rely solely on profits. Instead realize your business value. That value is in whether your business creates a solution to a problem or meets a need in society. Think critically about the value your new idea will add to society. Think in terms of tangible and intangible values. Does the value support your strategic direction or organizational goals and objectives? You also need to leverage on strategic partnerships to move your business forward. Forging strategic partnerships in the form of including qualified people to your team, well established companies to help support or mentor you, etc. are very helpful in boosting your business. Focus on identifying potential strategic partners who can help accelerate the idea forward. Strive to focus on their specific skills and availability. These are the very things that would propel your business forward. It is okay to have profit in mind; however, dwelling on the keys I have mentioned will help sustain your vision and mission in business.

Challenges

While we dream of starting huge businesses, challenges are bound to come. These challenges may be as a result of not meeting monthly or quarterly sales target, malfunctioning product on the market, insufficient resources, among others. These are actually stumbling blocks for improvement. Once you encounter such problems, know that it is an opportunity to change your strategy for something more engaging. If you were not able to acquire 100 customers within your first month of operation, instead of getting discouraged, it is very essential you try and change your sales techniques. Perhaps you were selling in a market that does not really need that type of product. Constantly learn from established entrepreneurs by reading wide, attending events, summits, and take part in competitions. They equip you with the requisite skills for your personal development. You should therefore eschew the notion that once you start your business, things automatically falls in place. Be prepared for hard knocks and developing of new strategies for your business from time to time.

Marketing Costs

Marketing your business can be relative depending on the type of product or services you are offering. However, no matter your product or service, you must endeavor to maintain focus on your target market. Is your product for kids, the aged, working population or for females?

It is important to focus more on your target audience than wasting funds on unnecessary ads which may go unnoticed by your target market. I highly recommend having a strong social media presence. However although your marketing strategy may reach a large audience, only a variable percentage of this group actually become your customers. Some may just fancy the marketing campaign of your product or service. It is prudent to focus on your target audience and make sales goals based on that demography. Sales is what brings you revenue, hence you should be very particular about which kind of market you are venturing into. Avoid the myth that you need a huge marketing budget for your startup. A winning strategy is to also focus on delivery because with marketing, you tend to create demand. Before you realize it, word about your product or service has spread far and wide.

Certain myths about starting a business can actually prevent you from building a sustainable and vision-driven company. However knowing what is right could give you a perfect experience on the entrepreneurial journey. Discard your preconceived views about running your business and move forward. It is possible! These experiences I've shared would at least clear some doubts about starting a business.

SUMMARY:

a) Start with the little that you have, either through personal savings, borrowing from friends among others.
b) Use Business models. They force you to go to the market quickly to test your assumptions. Every company is run by a team. A company will not succeed without the support of an able team.
c) Focus on adding value to society rather than mainly making profits.
d) Challenges may occur but you should see them as opportunities for making new strategies.
e) In marketing, your focus should be the target audience and how to meet their needs.
f) Build up your knowledge in running a business.

6 START SMALL

"Little by little, one walks far."- Peruvian proverb

Starting small can be very frustrating. In fact, it can make you quit even before you take the decision to begin. As you consider the limited resources you have, you will often get discouraged and think you cannot achieve your goals.

When I was a child one Ghanaian proverb I used to love; "nkakra nkakra na akoko de nom nsuo", literally meaning " the fowl drinks water one small sip at a time".

Individuals, organizations and nations have dreams, aspirations, wishes, and goals to achieve. It is not wrong to have them but how you begin and the steps you take can make a tremendous difference and a big impact on whether you will be successful or not.

Over the years, some businesses have craved so much for profit that they are ready to do everything, fair or foul to achieve the profit they desire. Staff salaries are slashed; exploitation of customers by way of making false promises, among other complex problems becomes the order of the day. Eventually this becomes their brand identity. Other companies even at the start of business build expensive and nice edifices just to entice customers. They open as many branches in different locations just to increase their customer base with the aim of making huge profits. In the end, you may earn the profits but customers may stop patronizing your products because you have not been fair to them. How can one start small to help place one's business on a great pedestal for success?

As already mentioned, most of the huge companies that we know of such as Microsoft and Apple started small. Even in other business industries, practitioners who started small have today grown bigger and better. Let me bring to bear some practitioners who started small and are now making sustainable progress, so that we can learn from them.

Professor Muhammad Yunus

Professor Muhammad Yunus started the Grameen Bank in his home country of Bangladesh with a loan of just £17, to lend tiny amounts of money to the poorest of the poor - those to whom no ordinary bank would lend. Most of his customers - as they still are - were illiterate women, wanting to set up the smallest imaginable village enterprises. It was his conviction that this new system of 'micro-credit', lending even such small sums, would give such people the spark of encouragement needed to pull themselves out of poverty. Today, Yunus's system of micro-credit is practiced around the world in some 60 countries, including the US, Canada and France. Grameen Bank is now a billion-pound business. It is acknowledged by world leaders and the World Bank to be a fundamental weapon in the fight against poverty.
A book, 'Banker to the poor', is Yunus's enthralling story of how he did it: how the terrible famine in Bangladesh in

1974 focused his ideas on the need to enable its victims to grow more food. It is a story of how he overcame the skeptics in many governments and among the practitioners of traditional economic thinking, and how he saw his micro-credit extend to even outside the Third World into credit unions in the West. HRH the Prince of Wales contributed a Foreword to the book, in which he hails Professor Yunus as 'a remarkable man [who] spoke the greatest good sense'.

Jonathan Swift

In the 1720s, Jonathan Swift began making small loans to "industrious tradesmen," who bound themselves to repay by offering cosigners rather than collateral. A century later, the Loan Fund system was widespread in Ireland.

At a point when we were selling a lot of things and making good monies, we were offered the opportunity to compete in the annual Junior Achievement company of the year program in 2010. We had to prepare a pitch for the judges of the competition. I recall there were judges from Barclays Bank Ghana, Fidelity Bank among others. It was a nerve racking experience but considering the fact that we had made a lot of impact with our project we were confident we would win something - We did! We were adjudged overall winners by the head Judge - Beatrice Odonkor of Barclays Bank and were selected to represent Ghana at the Africa competition in Nairobi. This was my first ever international journey and I was so excited about it. Before the trip we participated in management training with Barclays Bank and on one of the days we had lunch with the Group Managing Director, Ben Debrah. He advised us to be bold in our dealings and to never fear to fail. This is one of my most memorable experiences that I share when encouraging new business entrepreneurs. We finally got Nairobi and I was so amazed at the numerous things that the people of Africa were working on. There were so many mind blowing ideas and projects presented at the competition. As always, I tried to get to know others or make new friends and share experiences. I am very proud of the friends that I made over there and the fact that we are still in contact today amazes me. My hotel room mate Jesaya passed away in 2015 (May His Soul rest in perfect peace). I miss him so much because throughout the duration of the program he was constantly motivating me to do better and stay highly committed towards achieving excellence. We did not win the competition, but the contacts and networks that I made were enough to propel me towards the path of success. What we started as a small company had gone beyond the borders of Ghana.

I am sharing the above stories not to excite you but so that you would appreciate that starting small can make you progress in your business. You can learn other lessons from well performing businessmen and women in Ghana which I may not know but the fundamental principle of the personalities I described above is, they started small. Do not forget to start with the little resources that you have.

SUMMARY:

a) Starting with the little you have at your disposal does not only prevent incurring unnecessary costs but it also helps you avoid treating others unfairly in your bid to make it.
b) Starting small helps you to manage your little resources well, which encourages progress.

7 RESPONSIBILITY

"The moment you take responsibility for everything in your life is the moment you can change anything in your life."- Hal Elrod

What comes to mind when you hear the word 'responsibility'? Is it something that sends shivers down your spine or is it welcoming? Let me share a few thoughts with you. It is sometimes disheartening and sad whenever people blindly believe certain ideologies which are not true. One of such global ideologies that has contributed greatly in shaping the way we live is, not taking responsibility for one's actions and decisions in life. A significant number of people believe that whatever happens to them is by chance or that the universe planned it. Others go to the extent of blaming others for every 'bad' thing that occurs to them but the bottom line is that whatever happens to us, good or bad, is a result of the decisions we took in the past.

For example if someone is not excelling in exams, to the larger extent, it is not the teacher's laziness that caused their failure, neither is it the poor quality of study material that the lecturer gave out, but the onus should be on the individual who did not excel in the exams. If that individual decided to dedicate valuable time to study every day, he would have been successful. In many typical situations, people blame their inability to achieve certain goals on external factors that do not relate to their core business. We often hear that the management team is to blame for disorder in prices, low turnover, and a number of other negative conditions in a business. Thus, people deduce that management is the reason why a business may fail to meet its target. Rather the question should be this: What did employees do to avert that failure or how much did each employee contribute to that failure?

In most parts of the world, the problem of unemployment has taken center stage and each year people continually attribute the menace to the actions of external factors including the government. Instead of providing solutions to problems in their communities where they live to make some gains from that, they relax and expect things to happen within the twinkle of an eye. Most students the world over, graduate with a sense of entitlement to jobs and not the responsibility and urge to develop businesses with the skills acquired from the university. For me, the principle of taking responsibility of my actions in life shapes and guides the way I live in that I do not give up whenever I encounter opposition. I am aware that the results I reproduce are the consequences of my own decisions and actions and nobody else's. Thus, whatever my hands find to do, I put in my best effort, leaving little or no space for errors. I would rather spend my time improving upon my skills and competences than just throwing in the towel at the slightest difficulty.

One thing worth noting is that, entrepreneurship, in itself, is rewarding, if and only if you commit yourself to serving society. No matter how lonely the road may seem, I believe that there are a thousand and more problems people face on a daily basis that need quick solutions. Therefore, instead of dreaming of finding a good and decent job after graduating, it is always necessary to identify these problems and provide solutions to them. Others may argue that they require certain skills set in order to start their own businesses but actually the reverse is the case. You only have to be efficient and effective at whatever you plan to do as well as have some substantial amount of knowledge in the market or area of operation, as this would help in eliminating many errors and mistakes in the business.

I also believe that time wasted cannot be regained. Hence I try to do much with as little time as possible. This enabled me to believe in myself and use this confidence, zeal and boldness in me to achieve all goals. I take responsibility for my actions whether good or bad and that has made all the difference.

SUMMARY:
a) Take responsibility for your decisions and actions.
b) Entrepreneurship is rewarding if only you commit yourself into serving society.

8 WINNING TEAM

"Great things in business are never done by one person; they're done by a team of people."- Steve Jobs

To broaden my scope in business I read a lot of books about business operations and I also learnt a lot from successful people within my network. My first year in the university was met with intense pressure to study because I was pursuing one of the most difficult courses on campus - Economics, Mathematics, and Statistics. I barely had time for myself or for co-curricular activities like I used to, in secondary school. Things became tough and I had to find a remedy. Was I willing to throw away all the lessons I had learnt throughout my entrepreneurship journey or I was just going to focus on getting the best of grades out of the university? All my friends were focused on studying in the library in order to pass their exams. None of my friends thought about starting or running a business. One fateful evening I had a call from one of my old time partners about our projects. The call ended on a bad note because he was only looking at the challenges and why it will not work. I was very angry but in my anger, I challenged myself to start looking out for other opportunities. One major challenge in running successful businesses has to do with team management and I faced this hurdle often.

In order to cross this hurdle, it is important to establish a winning team. To a large extent the success or failure of your business depends on your team members. What kind of people do you have on your team and what amount of work are they doing on a daily basis? This is the most important aspect of running a startup. Note that nothing great is ever achieved without a winning team. One of the essential elements in the success of any startup company is the ability to create, enroll, and motivate a team around a vision. It is not good enough to have a great idea. You also have to be good at team development and the generation of collective action. Think through the talents you will require for starting and building your new company. As you think through and write down the types of talents you will be attracting, add names of specific people who can potentially fill these roles. Think about everyone you know because they may know someone who knows someone who would be perfect for your team.

There are three (3) critical Core Team members that make up the heart of any startup. Here is the kicker - as a founder it's likely you will be the only "beautiful" one. For the other two core team members, you will want to find people as beautiful as you are, at your core strength. This is not to say that you cannot hire people who are more creative than you are. If they will be good for your company, by all means, hire them. What are the skill sets of these three core team members? They are the Inventor, the financial manager and the promoter/sales manager.

The Inventor (Ideator): This is the person who comes up with new ideas for growing the business, invents new services and products with ease, and understands what customers want. This is the type of person who has an endless supply of ideas to turn into a business.

The Financial Manager This is the person who understands the business product or service and how to maximize revenue generating opportunities. Different from an accountant, this person is focused on how to creatively increase revenue.

The Promoter/Sales Person is like the PT Barnum of the world, who loves promoting an idea and can sell ice to an Eskimo! Selling and closing the deal comes naturally to this person. This is the type of person who is always looking for the next opportunity to make a sale. He or she should have a keen ability to pitch a compelling message.

The call I had that night unfortunately led to a misunderstanding between us. We barely understood each other. Sometimes when running a business you have to value your employees or partners, and have trust in them. I seriously felt intimidated that night and it all bordered on the interaction I had with my partner. Our relationships impact our businesses. Developing the right attitude in managing your team members has a direct link to achieving the set target and goals of the team. Moreover, you need to become a people collector. That is, you should be someone who establishes strong relationships with as many people as possible. Such people are as a matter of fact, highly skilled at networking socially, are "people connecters" and the go-to guy. For the rest of your life you may have to perceive each new person you meet as a potential team member that can help move your vision forward. You can never know when you will meet your next team member. Continue to add names to your potential team list and keep your mind and eyes wide open, ready to be a people collector.

It is important to note that startup funds are limited,

therefore do not make huge promises of paying your team members large salaries unless you actually have enough to cover a long period of about ten to twelve months. This is one of the issues that causes most startups to fail. As an Inventor, one thing you can do is to discuss expectations with your team members. Some may want to volunteer and learn more about the field of business. Hiring of volunteers is rare in Ghana and many parts of Africa, but it is a very affordable way to secure viable and valuable team members. Other team members may expect financial rewards in addition to gaining experience. Often some fail to realize that, a person devoting his time towards making a business a success is a cost in itself to him, and the owner of the business should be able to provide some compensation. One quick and affordable way to do this is to provide meals and transportation for the team members on a daily basis. This means you should have some amount of funds to cater for that. Be very honest with yourself at this stage as that is what would propel you to greater heights in your business. Another way out is for all team members to contribute towards a stock capital and each person entitled to equity. This is quite risky as all of you stand the risk of losing your initial capital. To avoid this is hard work and dedication. You really have to be disciplined and make huge sacrifices so as to achieve daily and weekly targets for your business. At this stage, you really do not have to mix friendship with business. Differentiate between friendships and business relationships and act accordingly. Business is serious matter.

It is very essential that the team lead coordinates the efforts of the other team members. There should be set targets for every day, week and month which will be compulsory for each team member. It is helpful to have a person responsible for monitoring the set objectives of the team and ensuring that they are achieved by the members within the duration specified. Such a person may be an advisor, counselor or even a consultant. These days, they are referred to as Subject Matter Experts (SME's). They may be in the technological field, creative, legal or marketing. These are not your team members, but people who believe in your concept and are willing to assist you in getting your business in shape. They are also called 'Mentors', because they stay with you for a long period to assist you in your day-to-day activities, to ensure that your objectives are clearly achieved. A legal mentor would assist in all legal aspects of your business. Creative and technological mentors would assist in your design and technological needs respectively. Coordinate these Mentors, and you are sure to make the best out of them.

SUMMARY:
a) In establishing a winning team you must remember that, to a large extent the success or failure of your business depends on your team members.
b) You must have the Inventor, the Financial Manager and the Promoter as part of your team.
c) Maintain good relationships with your team members.
d) Become a people collector.
e) Make an effort to be aware of the expectations of each of your team members so everyone is on the same page and no one gets disappointed if his/ her expectations are not met.
f) Ensure team members are treated right by providing compensation for sacrifices they make towards the success of your business.
g) Be honest with yourself when spending the funds of your start up.
h) Subject Matter Experts (SME's) are helpful in monitoring the set objectives of the team.

9 PRODUCTIVITY

"Start with good people, lay out the rules, communicate with your employees, motivate them and reward them. If you can do all those things effectively, you can't miss."- Lee Iacocca

I was very privileged to have landed an opportunity to serve as the Lead Organizer for the U.S. Department of State's StartUp Cup program in Ghana and Africa. To date it has been my favorite experience as an entrepreneur. It involved organizing business competitions, growing startups from scratch, pairing startups with mentors and business leaders in Ghana to help them achieve greater heights in business. Starting a business from scratch can be very hectic and what is more disturbing is making arrangements to have your staff or cofounders paid for their work in the company you started. This has accounted for the failure of most startups in recent times. The reason for the failure is not always because the founders do not have enough funding but also because of the challenge of paying the right amount for equal work done. What if performance does not match the amount paid or vice-versa? It has its own set of problems. In the past some companies devised ways of dealing effectively with this issue whilst others have just managed to bring their dream business to a standstill due to this challenge. Whatever the case may be, every business entrepreneur should know that no team member wants to work for free. How can a startup owner devise means of managing and compensating staff while achieving overall organizational goals?

Each individual wanting to join a startup or an SME (Small and Medium-Scale Enterprise) should note that, no employer or startup owner would select a person to join the company without considering the amount of output required of that person- which includes the number of hours of work per week. Employers usually look at the quantity, quality and intensity of a potential startup co-founder or team member before bringing him or her on board. The basic break down is the number of hours the individual is willing to or required to work (mostly dependent on the type of sector). Most technology startups require that you work long hours even throughout the night to ensure improved efficiency. The quality of the startup founder has to do with his/her degree of skills, not necessarily educational skills. On the job experience also counts significantly. If the individual is not willing to apply a significant degree of effort and time to the work assigned he does not become attractive to the company. If all these are satisfied, an individual is well on the road to becoming a potential cofounder or employee for a company or startup.

Ideally, a startup founder can reduce a bit of stress in managing the compensation of employees in two different ways - equity or employee benefits. The pre-investment stage of a startup is often the period which involves a lot of planning, market research and analysis as well as resource allocation. It also encompasses feasibility studies, subjecting projects to systematic scrutiny and quantitative reasoning. As a result, it is very difficult to really start paying out cofounders full amounts, which may limit finances that should be available for further prospects of the projects especially when starting off with personal savings. What I recommend is planning with partners or cofounders and striking a deal that will be witnessed by a third party.

Talking about equity, the bigger pie could be subdivided between the founders. For example, the Ideator could have 51% of total equity whereas other founders could have 10% each depending on the number of partners. The remaining could be reserved for investors and perhaps family members and friends who may have assisted you in one way or the other throughout the business cycle. Equity can be subdivided based on the amount of work expected from each person. For instance the greater the involvement the greater the percentage earned. Paying your partners or cofounders by way of equity is one way of ensuring that they provide full undivided attention to grow the business, knowing
that they are actually part owners of the startup. Another option available to the Startup owner is to pre-finance the expenses of the startup team members. This includes taking up their meals and transportation on a day to day basis as well as on-duty expenses. This is a way of motivating them to give off their best in order to achieve the goals of the company. Mind you, this should not continue for the long term. It should only form part of your short term plan. For instance, it could last for about one to three months, after which full salaries can be given to them.

Startups provide a very laudable opportunity to create jobs for economic growth in every country. The decision to start a business should be backed with plans for effective recruiting and efficient staff management. The earlier mechanisms are put in place to avoid employee issues, the better for the growth of the company. One way to ensure this is to have mentors assist you from the very onset of starting the business. Such mentors should necessarily be experts so that coaching you would not be a difficult thing to do. If you have the desire to begin a Startup, go for it! Let these keys guide you. You'd be creating more jobs and contributing towards the economic growth of your country. Such a commendable feat!

SUMMARY:

a) As an employer or Startup founder, you should consider the quantity, quality and intensity of a potential employee or partner before bringing him/her on board.
b) The employer must do his best to match the compensation of employees with employee productivity. This is why the quality of the team members employed must be considered in the hiring process.
c) The employer desiring to employ quality team members must know that no team member wants to work for free, and that various strategies such as pre-financing expenses of team members and equity benefits would serve as motivation for team members.
d) Your Startup could be someone's answered prayer for a job.

10 INTERPERSONAL RELATIONSHIPS

"Treasure your relationships, not your possessions."- Anthony J. D'Angelo

StartUp Cup became huge in Ghana and it seemed that everybody was talking about it. We had run successful competitions for some time. Startups including BraveHearts Expeditions, Davio Arts Center and Kawa Moka gave us testimonials for an impactful process. I had the chance to network with some of Ghana's finest business men and women throughout the program's lifespan and also network with a host of entrepreneurs and change makers.

One of such great personalities was Marina Langereis. She was a strong pillar to my business career. She aided in the planning of all aspects of my business through her company, Dutch Lady Consulting. She would always call me to advise me. Sometimes, she was stern concerning certain decisions I needed to make to progress in life. I would never forget the inspiration she gave me even in the sternness of her voice. As long as she was on the phone with you, you were certain to move a notch higher on your self-esteem ladder due to her constructive criticism and counsel. She was very instrumental in the first Startup Cup. She moved back to the Netherlands afterwards but returned to Ghana the following year to visit. It was then that she mentioned to me that she had been ill for some time and was receiving treatment at one of the best hospitals in the Netherlands.

In 2016, we launched the first ever Africa StartUp Cup competition where all winners from across Africa could compete for the African prize in Ghana. We sent out email newsletters and Marina managed to get in touch from her sick bed. She sent me a mail. It was her last and it will forever be a treasure:

Dear Emmanuel,

Thank you for your thoughtful reply. It warms my heart to read such words.

It is doing me well in this stage of my life.

I have very good memories of my time, energy and support I have dedicated to StartUp Cup.

I just received an email that Ghana is organising StartUp Cup Africa. Big hurray for the Ghana team of StartUp Cup. I was always convinced you would do well and do better every next episode.

I am sorry that I could not be part of these next episodes.

God guides me through everything. It all is like it is and I take it as it comes.

Do well for yourself, by that you will do well for others. I have seen you doing it, so I know you can.

Reach for the best, that is all you can do.

Thank you, you are in my heart,

Love,

Marina

May her soul rest in perfect peace! The importance of interpersonal relationships cannot be overemphasized. As long as there are people on the planet, we will have relationships be it good or bad. We need to become skilled in dealing with people. Stakeholders, internal processes, financial management other elements that aid efficiency and effectiveness have their foundations built on good people management. It is therefore critical to cultivate interpersonal skills that will facilitate your dealing with all kinds of people to ensure smooth relationships.

Effective relationships produce effective cooperation, coordination, team spirit, unity, peace and understanding. These outputs are necessary for the growth and development of individuals and organizations.

These six (6) interpersonal skills must be nurtured for effective business relationships and enhancing business operations.

Listening

To listen is to pay attention to what somebody is saying. It is very easy to be consumed by your thoughts, ideas, opinions and theories such that you inadvertently do not pay attention to others. This may result in you missing their great contributions or ideas. No matter how much you think you know you cannot know everything. It is important to allow others contribute to the process.

Listening to others does not mean they are better than you. It also does not mean you have nothing to contribute. It only affirms your decision to add more to the information you already have. This gives you added advantage over the one you are listening to. Bernard M. Baruch adds that 'most of the successful people I have known are the ones who do more listening than talking'.

In this regard, try to attend business seminars, meetings, conferences and also listen to business analytics and successful entrepreneurs on television and radio.

Ask Questions

A question is a sentence, phrase, or word that asks for information or is used to test someone's knowledge. Questioning as an interpersonal skill is closely related to the skill of listening. Asking questions helps clear any doubt you may have. It brings out ideas you may not have known. Ask your mentors, coaches, teachers etc. how they made it this far. Ask what their fears were. Ask what influenced the choice of their enterprise. Ask how they overcame their challenges. Ask about their failures and successes etc.

Shannon L. Alder says 'Most misunderstandings in the world could be avoided if people would simply take the time to ask, 'what else could this mean?'

Conflict Management

It grieves my heart to say that some enterprises have

folded up because of some strife among the Board, Management and staff. Team work has been dissolved due to strife or misunderstanding.

Conflict is inevitable. How one resolves or manages conflict is the key to success. As humans we have different ideas, goals, values, beliefs and needs. Since the entrepreneur often engages with people with different personalities, conflicts may occur as they may have different opinions on issues. Learning to manage conflict is integral to a high-performing team. Everybody can at the personal or professional level benefit from learning conflict management skills.

Typically we can respond to conflict by using one of these five (5) modes; competing, avoiding, accommodating, compromising and collaborating. None of these is wrong to use, but there are right and wrong times to use each (Algert, N.E & Watson. K.- 2002)

Servant Leadership

A boss I once worked for always took the blame when anything went wrong in the office. He praised us for what went right. He never glorified himself for team successes. This reminds me of how the disciples of Jesus were amazed when He washed their feet. They never imagined that the one they called Master and Lord would take the place of a servant!

Some entrepreneurs easily flaunt their achievements and make their subordinates feel so inferior as though they can never match them. This habit neither encourages initiative nor boosts the morale of followers.

Entrepreneurs who possess the skill of servant leadership always recognize the dignity of human beings. They treat others as they would want to be treated and set a good example for others built on truth, integrity and honesty. He is a source of energy, empathy and earned trust.

Networking

You can do it by yourself, I know! However, the truth is you cannot do everything by yourself. That is not an efficient way to live life or establish a business. You will definitely need the support of other people in certain areas. It is therefore necessary to cultivate the skill of networking with others in your field and other fields of business endeavors. Stay in constant touch with your partners, team members, board members and others you may come across in the course of running your business. Always be on top of your game in networking.

Benchmarking

The dictionary definition of benchmarking is to evaluate or check (something) by comparison with a standard. For instance you can measure an organization's policy, products, programs, strategies with those of another.

This is one skill I used to demonstrate back in school and I am sure most students do it. I often asked my colleagues who were good academically, the page or chapter they had reached in terms of course outlines or notes and their understanding of the content. Although it may be seen as a waste of time, it guided and encouraged me to put in more efforts in the areas of my studies where I was lagging behind.

Every entrepreneur needs to nurture these skills for continuous growth and development of his or her business. There are many successful business men and women in the market. From time to time it is wise to measure your performance against theirs to be sure you are on the right track.

It is said that if you want to go fast, walk alone but if you want to go far, walk with others. It is possible to make a positive impact as a start-up entrepreneur if you adopt these 6 interpersonal skills.

SUMMARY:

a) Build and maintain positive relationships with people you encounter within and around your business.
b) Be a good listener.
c) Ask questions.
d) Learn to resolve and manage conflicts appropriately.
e) A leader must know how to serve.
f) Engage in healthy comparisons to learn from the best.

11 GOAL SETTING MECHANISM

"Setting goals is the first step in turning the invisible into the visible."- Tony Robbins

Have you ever heard of the Sustainable Development Goals (SDGs) established by the United Nations (UN)? They are otherwise commonly known as the Global Goals. It is a universal "call to action" to end poverty, protect the planet and ensure that all people enjoy peace and prosperity.

These 17 Goals build on the successes of the Millennium Development Goals (MDGs) while including new areas such as climate change, economic inequality, innovation, sustainable consumption, peace and justice, among other priorities. The goals are interconnected – often the key to success on one will involve tackling issues more commonly associated with another.

The SDGs work in the spirit of partnership and pragmatism to make the right choices to improve life, in a sustainable way, for future generations. They also provide clear guidelines and targets for all countries to adopt in accordance with their own priorities and the environmental challenges of the world at large. The SDGs are an inclusive agenda. They tackle the root causes of poverty and unite us together to make a positive change for both people and planet. "Poverty eradication is at the heart of the 2030 Agenda, and so is the commitment to leave no-one behind," UNDP Administrator Achim Steiner said. "The Agenda offers a unique opportunity to put the whole world on a more prosperous and sustainable development path. In many ways, it reflects what UNDP was created for."

As an international advocate, +SocialGood Connector and a passionate executor of social change, I am always pleased to share how we can come together to achieve the SDGs by 2030. I founded Educational Communities Worldwide (Educom World), to promote a sustained global impact community of decent work and lifelong learning opportunities for all (SDG 4 & 8). Our mission is to harness the power of quality education in the fight against unemployment and skills gaps, primarily through sustainable tourism, knowledge transfer, and lifelong learning opportunities for all. I also co-founded Social Good Ghana to create online and on-ground activations for the SDGs. We have been very successful for a couple of years now in reaching thousands of youth. If we flash back to all the activities that I have been involved in, I would say, rather humbly, that I have been a backbone support for young people and entrepreneurs, providing them with all the resources that they needed to run a successful business, as well as creating employment opportunities for people in Ghana. It was not an easy road, but I devoted all my effort to invest towards making the world a better place. My achievements have been recognised by the United Nations Foundation, 2 Billion Under 20, Junior Achievement, Future of Ghana Top 30

Under 30 Awards among others.

As long as I can, I will continue to support efforts towards the attainment of the global goals. Here is a guideline for anyone who wants to help achieve the global goals. In as much as we want results by 2030, we must also be systematic in our approach towards the attainment of the goals. As you read further, you will find important information about connecting the goals to help achieve your organizational objectives.

Often we tend to think that goals and objectives are easy to set, and yet this notion is often wrong in the organizational context. Goals and objectives are difficult to set because we might not know what they should cover or because we lay out too many of them with the hope that we are covering all the bases. Similarly, goals and objectives can proliferate in organizations because new ones are set, while old ones are not discarded. Below are a few indicators of exceptional organizational goals:

1. Less is better. Concentrate on meeting the few key variables rather than the trivial many.

2. Measures created to meet goals should be linked to the factors needed for success—key business drivers.

3. Measures should include a mixture of the past, present and future to ensure the organization is concerned with all three perspectives.

4. Measures should be based around the needs of customers, shareholders, and other key stakeholders.

5. Measures should start at the top and flow down to all levels of employees in the organization.

6. Multiple indices can be combined into a single index to give a better overall assessment of performance.

7. Measures should be changed or at least adjusted as the environment and your strategy changes.

8. Measures need to have targets or objectives established that are based on research rather than arbitrary numbers.

I'd be happy to walk you through each of these criteria to help you gain a better understanding of these desirable characteristics of organizational goals and objectives. Ready? It is useful here to start by recognizing that goals, objectives, and measures are different things. As explained earlier, goals tend to be general statements, whereas objectives are specific and time bound. Measures are the indicators used to assess achievement of the objective. In some cases, a goal, an objective, and a measure can be the same thing, but more often you will set a goal, have a few objectives underlying that goal, and then one or more measures for each of the objectives.

Less Is More

Less is more. Less is better. Simple rules are the common mantra here. It is recommended that organizations adopt only one key goal and about two to seven set objectives. Such goals guide how the firm operates, identify which opportunities to pursue, set priorities, manage timing of actions and even inform business exit decisions.

If an organization adopts between two and seven key objectives, it helps one to accurately measure one's success. Here is the clue - managers should not try to follow no more than 20 measures of performance in terms of performance on objectives. Thus with two to seven objectives, and 20 performance measures, you will likely have a number of objectives somewhere between the number of set goals and the number of measures. Why this limit? "No individual can monitor and control more than twenty variables on a regular basis.

Tie Measures to Drivers of Success

One of the key litmus tests for setting goals, objectives, and measures is whether they are linked in some way to the key factors driving an organization's success or competitive advantage. This means that they must provide a verified path to the achievement of a firm's strategy, mission, and vision. This characteristic of effective goals, objectives, and measures is one reason that many managers use some form of Balanced Scorecard in their businesses.

The Balanced Scorecard process provides a framework for evaluating the overall measurement system in terms of what strategic objectives it contributes to. The big challenge, however, is to verify and validate the link to success factors. Managers who do not scrupulously uncover the fundamental drivers of their units' performance face several potential problems. They often end up measuring too many things, trying to fill every perceived gap in the measurement system.

Don't Just Measure the Past

For a variety of reasons it is important to capture past performance. After all, many stakeholders such as investors, owners, customers, and regulators have an interest in how the firm has lived up to its obligations. However particularly in the area of objectives and measurement, the best systems track the past, present and future. Echoing this observation, Robert Kaplan, co-originator of the Balanced Scorecard framework, published a book on the subject called The Balanced Scorecard: You Can't Drive a Car Solely Relying on a Rearview Mirror.

A combination of goals, objectives, and measures that provides such information is sometimes referred to as a dashboard—like the analogy above, a dashboard tells you how the car is running and through the windshield you can see where you are going. Indicators on how well the economy is doing, for instance, can suggest whether your business can experience growing or declining sales. Another leading indicator is customer satisfaction. General Electric (GE), for instance, asks its customers whether they will refer other potential customers to GE, based on the experience they have had with the company. GE's managers have found that the higher this likelihood of referral, the greater the next quarter's sales demands. As a result, GE uses this measure to help it forecast future growth, as well as evaluate the performance of each business unit.

Take Stakeholders into Account

While it is important to track the goals and objectives most relevant to the needs of the business, relevance is subjective. This is why it is valuable to understand who the organization's key stakeholders are and set the goals, objectives, and measures in such a way that all stakeholders can be satisfied or at the very least, stakeholders can gain information relevant to their particular interests. Some stakeholders may never be entirely satisfied with a company's performance - for example some environmental groups may continue to criticize a company's negative environmental impact, rather than being placated with more transparent reporting of what the company is doing on the environmental front. Similarly, stakeholders with social concerns will appreciate transparency in reporting on the organization's corporate social responsibility efforts.

Cascade Goals into Objectives

The less-is-more concept can apply to the way that goals cascade into objectives, which cascade into measures. Tying goals and objectives to drivers of success means that vision, mission, and strategy cascade down to goals, and so on. The first benefit of this cascade approach is that goals and objectives are consistent with the strategy, vision, and mission. A second benefit is that goals and objectives in lower levels of the organization are more likely to be vertically and horizontally consistent since they should be designed to achieve the higher-level goals and objectives and, ultimately, the overarching strategy of the organization.

Simplify

Information overload is a challenge facing all managers (as well as students and teachers). Using the method of simplification builds on the idea that managers can attend to a few things well but many things poorly. Simplification refers both to the use of fewer, not more, metrics, objectives and goals, and the idea that multiple measures should be distilled into single measures. For instance GE's use of the single question about referring customers is a powerful but effective leading metric that can be reinforced with its rewards system. When metrics involve multiple dimensions, in areas where the organization wants to gauge customer satisfaction, for example, a survey can have 10 or more questions. Think about the many customer satisfaction surveys you are asked to complete after making an online purchase. Which question is the most important? The challenge, of course, is that a simple average of the customer survey scores, while providing a simpler indicator, also may hide some key indicator that is now buried in the average score. Therefore, the organization might need to experiment a bit with different ways of simplifying the measures with the aim of providing one that best reflects achievement of the key objective.

Adapt

An organization's circumstances and strategies tend to change over time. Since goals, objectives and measures need to be in sync with the organization's strategy, they should be changed as well when the strategy changes. For example many U.S. automakers set out to dominate certain car and truck segments on the basis of vehicle features and price- not fuel efficiency. However, the recent fluctuations in oil prices gave rise to a market for more fuel-efficient vehicles. Unless the automakers set some aggressive fuel efficiency objectives for their new models, however, that is unlikely to be a differentiating feature of their cars and trucks. Adaptation of metrics is not the same as adding more metrics. In the spirit of fewer and simpler measures, managers should be asked to take a measure away if they plan to introduce a new one.

Base Objectives on Facts

Finally while goals may sometimes be general (such as performance goals in which managers simply state, grow profits by 10%), the objectives and the metrics that gauge them should be very S.M.A.R.T. (Specific, Measureable, Achievable, Realistic and Time Bound). Objectives should be based on facts and information, not intuition. A fact-based decision-making process starts with the compilation of relevant data about the particular goal. This in turn typically requires that the organization invests in information and in information-gathering capabilities.

For example, early in Jack Welch's tenure as CEO of GE, he set out a financial goal for the company of improving its Return on Assets (ROA), a measure of financial efficiency. One of the underlying determinants of ROA is inventory-turn, that is, how many times a firm can sell its stock of inventory in a given year. So to improve ROA, a firm will likely have to also improve its inventory turns. One of GE's divisions manufactured refrigerators and turned its inventory seven times per year. What objective should Welch set for the refrigerator division's inventory turn? Instead of simply guessing, Welch sent a team of managers into another manufacturing firm (with permission of the firm's owners and top managers) in a different industry and learned that it was achieving turns of 12 to 17 times per year! Armed with this information, Welch could then set a clear and fact-based inventory-turn objective for that division, which in turn supported one of the overarching financial goals he had set for GE.

Fact-based objectives can typically be clearer and more precise. The shorter they are, the relatively shorter time it will take to achieve them. For instance, a firm can likely predict next week's sales better than next year's sales. This means that goals and objectives for the future will likely need to be more specific when they are fairly current but will necessarily be less precise down the road.

The main challenge with fact-based objectives is that many firms find future opportunities in markets where no existing set of customers exist today. For instance before Apple released the iPhone how big had they expected that market to be? There certainly were no facts, apart from general demographics and the technology, to set fact-based goals and objectives. In such cases, firms will need to conduct "experiments" to learn about production and market characteristics, such that the first goals and objectives will be related to learning and growth, with more specific fact-based objectives to follow. Otherwise firms will only take action in areas where there are data and facts, which clearly creates a paradox for managers if the future is uncertain in their particular industry.

SUMMARY:

In making organizational goals:
a) Less is more
b) Don't just measure the past
c) Tie measures to drivers of success
d) Take stakeholders into account
e) Cascade goals into objectives
f) Simplify
g) Adapt
h) Base objectives on facts

12 MORAL INTEGRITY

"Food gained by fraud tastes sweet, but one ends up with a mouth full of gravel". (Proverbs 20:17)

It used to be that kindness, truthfulness, humility, peacefulness, support, contentment, hard work and all the other virtues you can think of were treasured qualities at the workplace, such that they were even a basis for praising, exalting or promoting others to higher positions. Sadly, that is not the case any more in many parts of the world.

Today people readily falsify documents to acquire loans and investments to expand their businesses; employees embezzle funds belonging to the company to set up their own business. Some would rather just wish to see their competitors collapse. The landlord is ready to cheat the tenant, and so too is the market woman who is ready to take undue advantage of her clients by charging very high rates. These acts have become so common that there is no shame in pursuing such unwholesome behaviors any more.

Why is this so? There are a number of factors driving these

behaviours. It can be attributed to the trappings of success; the desire to display wealth; the need to have what other people have and a society that values riches more than a good name, favours instant gratification over hard work; and economic downcast.

Let us take a closer look at these factors:

The Trappings of success

The armed robber who was not caught rejoiced for being successful at the burglary.

The business man who was able to maximize his profit also thanked God for this success. Everybody is yearning to succeed in their endeavors after all who wants to fail? No one!

The student wants to succeed in his examinations. Couples yearn for a successful marriage. The businessman wants to remain sustainable and successful. The pastor wants to grow his congregation. The driver wants more sales at the end of the day. Success is good but not when it comes through elements of fraud and other vices. Unfortunately, it appears the only thing society looks at these days is success and not the means for success. Today, the only way to be approved by society is to succeed in your field and so people are ready to use all means, fair or foul to get to the peak of any endeavour. In the field of international development, this tendency is called the Machiavellian traits. The person with this personality is basically cunning, scheming and unscrupulous, especially in politics or in advancing one's career.

Society has portrayed success in such a way that downplays virtues such as kindness, integrity, hard work, contentment and humility. We often see people awarded for various achievements but we do not often see rewards for moral virtues.

To the majority of people success means amassing all kinds of wealth and this determines the level of respect accorded you by society. So, what then is success? Is it the perception society has about amassing wealth or the ability to use fair or genuine means in the accomplishment of individual or organizational goals in life? Albert Einstein helps us out by stipulating and I quote: "Try not to become a man of success but a man of value." It simply means we must try to eschew all manner of evil ways, in our efforts to accomplish our goals, be it in the area of business, relationships or career.

The Desire To Display One's Wealth

Often some wealthy people ostentatiously show off their riches. This has been typical of some sports people, actors or conglomerate owners. This behavior is often evident in their utterances where they showcase their wealth on social media and television appearances. This behaviour pattern is as a result of a primal human need for approval and to feel more superior. It also represents a deep seated need to be remembered even after they are dead and gone. However the sad part we must bear in mind is some of these wealthy persons acquired their riches through foul or corrupt means.

The Need to Have What Other People Have

The eye of man is never satisfied. Today we want one thing and tomorrow we desire a different thing including what others have. This is pure greed because society has become so competitive that many feel left out or successful if they do not have what others possess and display. Sometimes we lose our self-esteem when we cannot match up with the achievements of others. Therefore some are willing to give up their morals just to have what others have. Some will back bite others, may even kill or wish their friends dead. In other cases many have become unnecessarily displeased with their own achievements and cheat during exams or.

A Society That Favours Instant Gratification Over Hard Work

Few will ask how you got what you have but many are and will be unaware as to what you went through before getting where you are. Many think you are an overnight success and prefer to adopt the 'short-cut' model of achieving the same success they see you enjoying. The driver refuses to join the long queue of cars and finds another route to reach his destination or even tries to overtake others who are waiting patiently in the queue. In Ghana some students refuse to study but prefer to seek the exam questions illegitimately in what is popularly referred to in the local parlance as 'going for Apo ', in order for them to pass. At the workplace some employees have affairs with their bosses for a promotion while others betray their colleagues to seek favours and recognition. What about the athlete who resorts to performance enhancement drugs or the coach who secretly connives with the referee for a favour. Eventually we see such persons on top and think they got there by dint of hard work. Gradually these acts are becoming so normal that society finds no shame in these acts.

Economic Downcast

'Charley, the economy hard oo! We for find wanna way through oo'. This is a common statement amongst some youth of this country. It literally means, 'the economy is tight, therefore we need to use any means to make a living". Anaman Pauline & Armah Ernest in their writing on Sex, Gender and Corruption in Ghana said "we should not be kidding ourselves; times are hard and if you are not careful you may overstep your bounds to engage in illegalities to be able to survive. That should not be justified in anyway." These words are indeed very true. However how many people will be willing to adjust?

How can the start-up entrepreneur create value through personal moral integrity? The start-up entrepreneur cannot be left out on matters of personal moral integrity. They will be faced with the various facets of the economic downturn and be naturally tempted to show off their wealth with time. They may also be tempted to have what others have. This notwithstanding, the start-up entrepreneur needs to be aware that real value, true greatness, real success and achievement lies in practicing moral integrity.

SUMMARY:
a) Moral integrity is hardly regarded these days.
b) The trappings of success; the desire to display wealth; the need to have what other people have, a society that values riches more than a good name, instant gratification over hard work; and economic downcast are the causes of the loss of moral integrity.
c) Success is good but not when it comes through elements of fraud and other vices.
d) It appears the only thing society looks at these days is success and not the means for success.
e) We must try to eschew all manner of evil ways, in our efforts to accomplish our goals.

13 JOB CREATION

"Entrepreneurship, entrepreneurship, entrepreneurship. It drives everything: Job creation, poverty alleviation, innovation."- Elliot Bisnow

While discussing productivity, we agreed that starting a business from scratch is challenging and has many processes involved. The challenges most often lead to the collapse of startups even before they are birthed. For many of the collapsed startups it is not because the founders do not have enough funding but the ability to having the right team who are skilled to perform well is the challenge. If they succeed, however, startups will be very critical to economic growth.

Startups provide a very laudable opportunity to create jobs which is critical to any nation's economic growth. The decision to start a business must come with plans for sustainability, productivity, effective recruiting and efficient staff management. The earlier mechanisms are put in place to avoid employee issues, the better for the growth of the company. One way to ensure this is to have mentors assist you from the very onset of starting the business.

Such mentors should necessarily be experts so that coaching you wouldn't be a difficult thing to do.

Many recent reports suggest that startups, young, fast-growing companies create most new jobs during economic expansions, as is evident in a new report which summarizes recent research on the dynamics of job creation.

"Startups" are firms in their first year of existence. They play a critical role in job creation, according to analyses of recently developed federal data by economist John Haltiwanger and his colleagues.

Policymakers often think of small business as the employment engine of the economy, but when it comes to job-creating power, it is not the size of the business that matters as much as it is the age. New and young companies are the primary source of job creation in the American economy. Not only that, but these firms also contribute to economic dynamism by injecting competition into markets and spurring innovation (See The Importance of Young Firms for Economic Growth By Jason Wiens and Chris Jackson).

The oft-quoted American sports slogan is "Winning isn't everything. However, "It's the only thing," could well be attributed to the economic importance of firm formation in creating jobs. A relatively new dataset from the U.S. government called Business Dynamics Statistics (BDS) confirms that startups aren't everything when it comes to job growth. They're the only thing. This excerpt is from the July 2010 Kauffman Foundation Research Series: Firm Formation and Economic Growth paper The Importance of Startups in Job Creation and Job Destruction.

Put simply, this paper shows that without startups, there

would be no net job growth in the U.S. economy. This fact is true on average, but also is true for all but seven years for which the United States has data going back to 1977.

So, let us create more jobs through startups so we contribute towards the economic growth of the country.

14 NEW YEAR DECEPTION

"Character is the ability to carry out a good resolution long after the excitement of the moment has passed."- Cavett Robert

Every New Year we can all attest to the fact that almost everyone makes New Year's resolutions. However, setting these big goals only resulted in grave disappointment as most never materialise.

What plans did you make at the beginning of the previous year and how many of those plans did you achieve at the end of the year? In this chapter we will discuss some of the reasons why you may not have realized your previous year's goals and further highlight more efficient ways of ensuring business success

New Year's resolutions are the norm. Everyone makes these declarations privately or publicly. Despite your area of expertise, it seems to be one of the tools which is widely practiced to ensure that we stay on course to achieve our career or business goals. Sadly, New Year resolutions appear to be deceptive as we go through each year without accomplishing much on the list. I have discovered a few reasons why this is so. The key tip is that one needs to focus intently on achieving that resolution or goal. In many cases you have to go the extra mile and make huge sacrifices.

New Year resolutions give you false hope and tend to make you lazy. Out of the excitement of the New Year we are blinded to reality. We make huge plans without accounting for the energy, skills and conviction needed to implement those resolutions.

Let me shed some light on a few reasons why some New Year's resolutions often fail:

• They are not specific. We say "I want to increase personal investments and savings this year" but when faced with the birthday parties in March, the smart phone releases in June, and the music shows in August, that goal falls by the wayside. You need to focus on one particular thing while making sure that you take steps to achieving them systematically.

• They are unrealistic. "I want to build the biggest bank in Ghana." Really? You do not even have a "susu" company or have the basic knowledge about how banks operate. Setting unrealistic, difficult-to-achieve goals is a quick way to guilt and failure.

• They are based on willpower, not systems. We say, "I want to increase the customer base" instead of going to the field to convince buyers. We say, "I want to acquire a Master's degree" instead of testing different universities or colleges to find out which best suits your career goals. In short, what systems have you put in place to ensure that your goals are achieved? Focus on your monitoring systems.

Here are a few areas you might want to consider if you really want to make something out of your New Year resolutions. You may have achieved just 5% of your 2017 resolutions in business but there is still room to achieve more. Here are my two cents:

- **Social Aspects** - The area of goal-setting revolves around gaining new customers within your business as well as developing new ways to engage those customers. It is very essential that you communicate often with your customers to know their changing taste in order to give you an upper hand in developing new trends to meet their needs. It is always best to anticipate your customers' evolving needs rather than wait for them to start complaining about your product or service. Social goals also cover the measure of impact that you will have on society. Do you create a Corporate Social Responsibility (CSR) budget for your company or your only interest is to make more than enough sales on each passing day? It is essential to contribute to the development of the society where you operate your business. It contributes massively to the image of your company. Investing more time in the social aspects of your business helps in shaping your company's goals and visions for a longer time period. It is the CSR plans of some businesses that make them offer services such as Free Health Screening, Mobile Libraries, Food Banks, sponsor Homeless Shelters or soup kitchens in their communities.

- **Political Influence** - Another area worth considering in your country of operation has to do with the level of political stability. A poor political environment could have adverse effects on your business. Develop your product or build your business with the current or future political environment in mind as an external factor. This ensures that you are highly alert on the full life cycle of the business. For companies hoping to expand operations to other countries aside their host country this is an important consideration for your success. It is also important to consider the current policies within the country with respect to the kind of business that you are doing.

- **Economic Influence** - Economic goal-setting has to do with activities that help to gain an understanding of the processes that govern the production, distribution and consumption of goods and services in your country. As a business leader you must always be up to date on certain economic aggregates such as the level of inflation, taxation, interest rates, among other factors. These aggregates contribute to the macro and microeconomic structure of every economy. A better understanding of these, can lead to favourable or less favourable business results for your company.

- **Religious factors** - Although everyone has different beliefs and religious affiliations no single individual should force a coworker to believe in something that goes contrary to their religious beliefs. Condemnations on the basis of religious beliefs are unacceptable in the work place. Instead of being judgemental of other workers' religious background, it is always important to ask yourself how best you can collaborate with each other on a particular assignment or task so as to learn from each other. Being judgemental breeds discord and may create negative results in the attainment of company goals and objectives.

- **Morale** – Each year, companies spend millions just to keep the morale of their workers high in other to achieve the maximum results at work. It is observed that anytime a worker is motivated, he or she is able to produce exactly what is needed for the organization to grow.

Managers need to provide incentives satisfactory enough to compel workers to put in their best at work.

In a nutshell consider these factors in your year-end planning for the upcoming year. The previous year may have shown negative or discouraging results in your business but I believe if you consider these points, you will soon be making headway in bringing out the best in your organization.

SUMMARY:

a) Businesses fail to meet their New Year resolution because they are unrealistic, they are not specific and they are based on willpower not systems.

b) In order for a business to meet its New Year resolution it should consider Social aspects which involves undertaking Corporate Social Responsibilities, as well as liaising with stakeholders on the basis of political, religious and economic issues , and boosting the morale of employees.

15 BECOME A "USAIN BOLT" START UP

"Be Reasonably Ambitious and Not Competitive"

This man, the Jamaican athlete called Usain Bolt is really a delight to watch during athletic competitions. Any time I watch him run, I wonder how he is able to move and win all his races. I am sure I am not the only one curious about his success because even the competition organisers go the extent of making him undergo several tests to be sure his stellar success is not boosted by 'performance-enhancing drugs'.

In one of his interviews, he exclaimed that 'For me I am focused on what I want to do. I know what I need to do to be a champion, so I am working on it.' He added "if I get to be a legend, I have achieved my goal." Hear this last statement from him "there are better starters than me but I am a strong finisher".

After hearing him out, one lesson I drew was that Usain Bolt was reasonably ambitious and not competitive. He stated himself he was not the greatest starter as there were others better than him, but he was a strong finisher. It is not how you start, but how you finish. What a revelation! This is one trait that start-ups need to adapt in order to be legends in their chosen fields. Start the business but finish well. But the question is how did Usain adopt this trait? Pondering over his words, I drew some insights which I would like to share as best practices for start-ups.

To be reasonably ambitious, you must identify your priorities. If you do not know what is important to you, you will settle for everything and anything whether meaningful or meaningless, purposeful or purposeless, beneficial or unbeneficial, befitting or unbefitting, helpful or not helpful, relevant or irrelevant. In the end you get confused! This is one reason some start-ups do not go far as they pursue businesses for which they do not have the appropriate capacity to manage. I know you have a number of business ideas, but can you roll them all at the same time? This supports the Akan traditional adage, "no matter how hungry you are you cannot eat with both hands." Usain Bolt had a lot of dreams which included playing soccer and becoming an athlete but he chose to be an athlete for now. Take your time and identify and prioritize which business idea you are most passionate about and have what it takes to pursue it.

The greatest people in history had many failures. This again emphasizes what Usain implied: How you finish is better than how you start. Certainly, we remember these individuals as success stories and we treat those stories as legends and those individuals as gods. But each of them failed epically and repeatedly, more so than the combined successes of all of humanity.

Secondly, you must have a goal. Indeed it is true that if you do not know where you are going, every road seem to lead you to your destination. However, two features of a good goal are that it they must be real and achievable so you do not become over-ambitious. This may cause you to retreat or give up when you do not get there. My point is set realistic and achievable business goals in your efforts to begin a start-up enterprise.

Additionally, you must focus on your strengths and build on them.

What are you good in; handling money, persuading people, negotiation, organising events, cleaning, decorations, drawing, painting, coaching, restoring calm, conflict resolution and
mediation etc. One problem I have identified with many start-ups is that we tend to allow what we are not good at to block our strengths. We allow our weaknesses to discourage us. Usain Bolt highlighted his strength as being a 'strong finisher' and he made good use of that.

Study your competitors but do not copy them. Competition can be destructive if not done in a healthy way. Research shows that some micro-finance companies collapsed as a result of unhealthy competition amongst 2nd Tier micro-finance companies. They were tried to be at par or rock shoulders with the rural banks, savings and Loan companies. In trying to compete, you will definitely compare. Although enterprises look the same, they are different in terms of capacity, mission and vision. You should therefore be careful as a start-up as you will find competition in your chosen field. Usain Bolt was faced with competition but he focused on his goal.

The last insight I want to share with you is to pursue a business you are passionate about. Passion drives innovation, endurance and excellence. Research has also shown that any establishment which is not backed by passion of the Board and Management does not go far. Many Start-up managers will easily fold their hands in despair especially in times of crisis if there is no passion. As you start your business, be sure to start with passion.

Now, let us put these into practice. Become a "Usain Bolt" startup.

SUMMARY:

a) In order to be reasonably ambitious, you must identify your priorities.
b) Have a goal, know where you're going.
c) Focus on your strengths and build on them.
d) Study your competitors but do not copy them.
e) Pursue a business you are passionate about.

16 YOU MAY FAIL AND SO WHAT?

"If something is important enough, you should try, even if the probable outcome is failure"-- Elon Musk

I believe the word 'failure' will never be dreamt of by most Start-ups. Success is all we wish for. Indeed, this must be so, for who wants to fail, nobody! Nonetheless, failure should not stop you from even trying.

It is easy to see successful entrepreneurs and think they were born that way or never failed. The reality was that most of them were ambitious and relentless. Again, in life we cannot run away from failure. This is not a license to consciously fail. What matters most is our ability to deal with it when it comes our way whether it was caused by our negligence or not. I am yet to find entrepreneurs who can boldly assert that in the lifetime of their business operations, they never experienced failure.

Maya Angelou was asked the secret of her success in business. This is what she said "you may encounter many defeats, but you must not be defeated. In fact it may be necessary to encounter the defeats, so you can know who you are, what you can rise from, how you can still come out of it."

The world of business is full of uncertainties; political influences, depreciation of the cedi, technological advancement, and unhealthy competition within a business industry all of which may force your business to go under. Some businesses have folded up as a result of technological advancement. Remember how mobile phones rendered the then telecommunication centre businesses irrelevant.

Michael Jordan is one of the greatest basketball players of all time. But he often shares his profile in failure. He openly talks about how many times he failed and did not make the playoffs. His story is another great example of how to finish well by turning your failures or slow starts into success. He said: "I've missed more than 9000 shots in my career. I've lost almost 300 games. 26 times, I've been trusted to take the game winning shot and missed. I've failed over and over and over again in my life. And that is why I succeed."

Failure is a humbling exercise, both for the observer and the observed. But learning is a humbling process so learn rather to finish well after you start.

The question is, what would you do if you find your company in shambles? Below are three steps you can take.

First and foremost simply calm your nerves.

It is a very disturbing moment I know. The heat, tension, aggressive posture of clients, the threatening statements, insults from clients, and the sleepless nights can be very unbearable. In all of these, we must learn to calm your nerves. Let us not heed to the pressure from friends, clients, stakeholders. Doing so may land you into more distressed situations. Some Directors have committed suicide as a result, which is really unfortunate. Let us remember that pondering over the distressed situation when you feel under pressure cannot solve the situation. It only blocks your ability to reason more accurately.

Assessing the cause of failure

In fact it serves as a building block on which you can restore your company in the near future as you learn from them. Was the failure due to wrong application of business model, inadequate planning, lack of expertise and skill to operate and manage a company, over reliance on creditors, absence of efficient governance structures, weak internal control structures resulting in fraud, unhealthy competitions, weak regulatory framework etc.

Re-Strategize

After assessing the cause of the failure, it is time to re-strategize. It is now time to ask these vital questions:

1. Do I intend to operate the same business again?
2. Do I move and set up other business opportunities available?
3. Do I have what it takes to set up that business?

In fact re-strategizing is a herculean task, but you need not give up. Start small and gradually build the new strategy. One way is to brainstorm with your team or seek ideas from other professionals in your field. Your ability to identify the cause of your business failure could lay a solid foundation to finding sustainable solutions. If the collapse was due to inadequate planning, it is prudent to seek the services of a strategic planning expert or consultant. I can recommend a few if you contact me directly. If the failure was over reliance on creditors for capital, it is time to start small for example with available and existing resources such as your savings.

Do not let the fear of failure keep you from even trying your hands on a business venture. Remember the words of Elon Musk "If something is important enough, you should try, even if the probable outcome is failure". Be bold and keep moving forward!

SUMMARY:

a) As an entrepreneur, do not be afraid to fail.
b) Failure is a humbling exercise while learning is a humbling process.
c) When you fail, first calm your nerves, next, assess the cause of failure and then re- strategise.

17 MAKE SOUND FINANCIAL DECISIONS

"We had enough money but, I do not know where it all passed. Our company is really broke!"- Distressed Director of a Microfinance Company".

Human beings are decision makers. We make decisions all the time. We decide on issues concerning our health, relationships, education and more. Institutions and nations are no exception when it comes to decision making. However we must be cautious because the decisions we make can be beneficial or harmful.

One area of human life that can really cause discomfort when not handled properly is financial decisions. According to a Management Study Guide, financial decision is an important function which a financial manager must perform. A sound financial decision is one which aims at maximizing shareholders return with minimum risk.

Company needs differ according to the size and type of

business, but the areas of financial decision making remain the same. Ultimately, every company must ensure that it makes good use of its finances in order not to run into debt or liquidity problems.

It is worthy to note that bad financial decisions can cripple even big, capital-rich corporations over time. Microfinance Companies are no exception. Nonetheless, companies that make sound financial decisions continue to enjoy long term business operations.

It is with this background that I write to introduce microfinance practitioners to the skills in making sound financial decisions. These notes were taken from the library of Econet Wireless from Zimbabwe which I wish to share with you. In order to make sound financial decisions, the following points can be helpful to your company.

Create a cash flow budget

A cash flow budget helps to ensure that you can comfortably cover all potential expenses. It enables you to manage your revenues and expenses proactively. It is important to keep your cash flow budget up-to-date and make sure it reflects changes in your operating environment.

Know the sensitivities in your cash flow

It is important to pin down which items - incomes or overheads - will have the most impact on your cash flow. Fees and charges for example, have a significant impact on your cash flow, yet is difficult for you to change. At the same time, competitive pressures may prevent you from increasing them.

Manage the credit you are extending to your customers

There are a number of different ways to improve how you manage your receivables.

Establishing effective credit policies is an important part of extending credit to customers.

You might also think about how you can encourage clients to pay more quickly. For example, consider discounts for early payments or charge interest on accounts that are past due.

While interest and late charges may actually become a source of income for your business, it is important to apply some due diligence. Extremely late payments are more likely to become write-offs and will also keep some of your working capital tied up.

Keep your Payables Up-to-Date

Regularly reviewing your accounts payable schedule helps determine how well you are keeping up with your credit obligations. A useful practice is to have an "aging schedule" which shows you how much you owe, to whom, and whether you are current or past due on any bills.

Reduce expenses

Look for ways to cut back: for example, can the cost of promotional materials (such as printing or production) be reduced without compromising their quality and impact?

When your business volume expands bring in temporary, contract, or part-time help before committing to additional full-time staff.

An independent audit may also be helpful in revealing redundancies and inefficiencies that you can address.

Use credit effectively

The best credit facility will depend on your company's individual circumstances, business plans, and existing credit facilities.

For example, term loans are ideal for long-term capital purchases, while lines of credit can be used to meet short-term working capital requirements or to take advantage of unexpected business opportunities.

Put your Company's Surplus Cash Flow to Work

Assess how much money you need to set aside for emergencies. To do this, review your company's cash flow history for any patterns.

Also consider how potential changes in the economy, such as currency or interest rate fluctuations could affect your revenues or expenses.

Any surplus in your cash flow can be used to pay off debts, or to maintain a certain level of working capital.

I wish to conclude by also sharing this story by Econet Wireless:

"I recently read a report which showed that many working professionals in a major European country, have enough savings to last 18 days, if they ever lost their jobs! The

squirrel, a small animal that collects nuts during the

summer, for the long winter, would no doubt be quite amused.

A business associate, who ran a construction company, came to me once complaining bitterly that people were stealing from him. He pointed out that he had done huge projects, in the past, and yet he was now totally broke. "How could this be"?!

" The problem is if I tell you, the truth, I will lose you as a friend." I told him. "Please, please tell me!" He begged. Okay:

To start with, always, always remember that, it is harder to hold onto money, than to make money. Teach it to your children, if nothing else.

People who inherit businesses, or money, generally end up losing everything. The first thing you need to know is when you are making money, and when you are not. A large turnover, or revenue, does not mean you are making money.

Then I said to him, "before you tell me, how much you made on this project, and that, let us talk rather about how much you saved, from what you made on each project."

Then he looked at me, with a bemused almost blank look on his face.

Then after a while, he said, "I made investments".

I looked at him, in the eye, and said, "You know it is not true. You bought a nice car, you built a nice house, you..... You did not invest in your capacity to make more money and you did not SAVE, for the rainy day."

Then I said, "do you want us to carry on, this discussion; it could become very painful for you?"

He looked down on the ground.

I stopped.

Friends, if you have a job, any job; no matter how little you make: SAVE something.
If you are running a business, no matter, how small: SAVE something".

SUMMARY

a) We must be cautious when making financial decisions, because the results may be beneficial or harmful

b) Sound financial decisions are those that aim at maximizing shareholders return at the same time minimizing risk

c) The process of making sound financial decisions involves:

-Creating a cash flow budget

-Knowing the sensitivities in your cash flow

-Managing the credit you are extending to your customers

-Keeping your payables up to date

-Reducing expenses

-Using credit effectively

RISE ABOVE

-Putting your company's surplus cash flow to work

d) Always remember to save for the rainy day

18 BE SKILLFUL AT WHAT YOU DO

"It is possible to fly without motors, but not without knowledge and skill."-Wilbur Wright

Have you wondered why the lion is the king of the forest? Have you wondered why some soccer players are preferred to others? Have you wondered why some companies continue to stay strong in spite of economic turmoil? This is simply because of the skills they possess.

The benefits of possessing set skills in whatever you do cannot be underestimated. The policeman, petty trader, nurse, engineer, teacher, lawyer, student, house help, husband, wife all need skills in order to perform creditably in their various disciplines. The microfinance practitioner is no exception.

It is not surprising that one of the factors that led to the collapse of some microfinance companies was the inadequate and lack of skills of most personnel of these companies.

According to the Macmillan Dictionary, a skill is the ability to do something well.

Being skillful injects confidence in you. You are not deterred by any difficulty that may come your way because you understand what it takes to overcome them. It makes you stand out among the lot. Ultimately, you often perform well in whatever you do. These tools will be helpful in building your skills:

Acquire Knowledge

Knowledge and skills are interconnected. Without knowledge, you cannot acquire skills. It is therefore very important to acquire knowledge in whatever you do or intend doing. Attend courses in areas you wish to gain knowledge. Participate in seminars. Read books on your areas of interest. Listen to tapes, CDs that teach or provide some information on the areas you wish to be skillful at.

Do not stop Practicing

The late Bruce Lee, a martial artist once said "I fear not the man who has practiced 10,000 kicks once, but I fear the man who has practiced one kick 10,000 times." Constant practicing of what you learn is one sure way of acquiring skills.

Use Communication and Information Technologies

Making good use of technology can go a long way to helping you acquire the needed skills in what you do. Today there are a lot of resources on the internet that teach you how to do what.

Attend Skills-Oriented Training Programs

Take advantage of the numerous training programs held in

colleges, training centres and institutions. These programs provide learners with a hands-on practical knowledge and experience in their chosen disciplines.

Keep Asking Questions Relevant to Your Field.

The more you ask, the more you know and the more you know the greater your chances of developing skills in that discipline. Never hesitate to ask questions from people who are skilled in the areas of your discipline.

Let us test your skill in the following disciplines. Using the scale of 1, 3 and 5 (where 1 represents Not at All, 3 represents Somehow and 5 represents Highly Skilled), indicate your strength in that discipline and take the needed action to get trained.

Remember, knowledge is power but skill is mighty power.

	DISCIPLINE	CIRCLE ANSWER		
1	Ability to monitor loans	1	3	5
2	Ability to market products and services	1	3	5
3	Ability to access and manage funds	1	3	5
4	Ability to prepare microfinance financial reports	1	3	5
5	Ability to negotiate	1	3	5
6	Ability to manage lending methodologies	1	3	5
7	Ability to manage liquidity	1	3	5
8	Ability to	1	3	5

	handle customer complaints			
9	Ability to strengthen internal controls	1	3	5
10	Ability to manage depositors funds	1	3	5
11	Ability to analyse and interpret financial reports	1	3	5
12	Ability to manage loan delinquency	1	3	5
13	Ability to develop business plan.	1	3	5
14	Ability to use microfinance software	1	3	5
15	Ability to	1	3	5

	recover loans			
16	Ability to develop products and services	1	3	5
17	Ability to manage working capital	1	3	5
18	Ability to prepare and control a budget	1	3	5
19	Ability to conduct credit appraisal	1	3	5
20	Ability to make investment decisions	1	3	5

SUMMARY:

a) Being skillful helps to boost your confidence

b) An entrepreneur can develop his/her skills by acquiring knowledge, constant practice, using communication and information technologies, attending skills oriented training programmes, and asking questions.

19 VISUALISING

"Unless you know where you are going then you will not know how to get there."- Stephen Richards

This In order to be successful in setting up a successful business startup, one must dispel the myths and misconceptions. Get it out of your system because we all know we are what we think.

Visualisation is a great tool which helps me daily to plan effectively towards amazing personal and professional achievements. In order to properly map out your progress in life and business, visualization techniques are helpful.

Simply put, visual techniques actually simplify the entrepreneurial journey. It helps you make quick amendments to your plans. It also gives you the full picture of what you need to do to become a successful startup. One such tool is the BUSINESS MODEL DESIGN™ that we used in the Startup Cup process.

The Business Model Design is a one pager business model.

A quick glance at the scorecard makes it easier to actually focus on the most important things only. It also supports going to the market quickly and testing assumptions. It helps to secure customers and generate revenue as quickly as possible. Your goal therefore as an entrepreneur with a new business concept is to identify a new business model, test assumptions, secure customers and evolve your model as you grow revenue and market share. I will share with you how the Business Model Design is done.

Your Big Idea/Value Proposition
Step 1 on your Business Model Design should be about value proposition. The value you are providing to customers should be something worthy, satisfactory, efficient, of high quality and above all should be the answer to someone's most pressing need. It is also possible that the product or value that you are providing is actually something that already exists in the market. You would have to devise ways to ensure what you are providing adds greater value than what your competitor has. Provide a reason for people to purchase your product or service. For instance you can go the extra mile. Instead of simply making the product available in the store, offer to deliver directly to the customer's home. This value in Ghana would be much appreciated.

Customer, Product, Market and Vehicle
Step 2 should be about CUSTOMER development because that is the most important part of starting and generating revenue from your business. You should have a target market for which your product or service is unique and clearly identifiable in your marketing promotions. It cannot be over emphasized that there should be a compelling reason why anyone should purchase your product or service. This means more work has to go into the design aspect of the final product you are offering to the market. Being a small company with limited resources

and skills, it is very essential to target your customers so you can be able to go to the market and generate revenue as quickly as possible.

Be concerned about the PRODUCT. How are you going to design the final product or service so as to make it more attractive to the customer? In effect what are you selling? It is essential to be more specific on this! This step also helps you address your market. How big is your market size? What is the growth potential of your product or service? If there are similar offers on the market, you really need to strategise to be able to beat the market in terms of sales revenue.

VEHICLE means that you need to decide which possible channel you would be using to get to your customers. Are you going to use the internet or you are going to rely on personal sales, distributors, etc. The methodology or channel of getting your product to the market is important in determining how well or poor you will sell your product or service.

It is very necessary to visualize your way out to a better startup and this model helps with that process. This helps to reduce the various workload to make moving forward a sure bet. Whether you run a day job or you are a young graduate, there is no perfect time to start a business than now.

The art of visual thinking does not required one having any skill in art or drawing. You just need to clarify your goals and make your startup goals more achievable, it is essential that you sketch your way through the startup journey.

Drawing Out Your Best

When visual thinking don't think too hard about what you are drawing. Let the sketch be natural, intuitive and straight from the heart going with the flow of your consciousness. Focus your thinking, energy and drawing on the problem to be solved or new idea. For example, if your business idea is about starting a water supply business so as to reduce water shortage in your community then you may be visualizing and sketching a water reservoir, water supply tanks, water tubes, transporting the water to the community, revenue stream from each water supply. Once sketched on your drawing book it can be tremendously helpful in getting 80% of the work done.

Some things to think about as you start the visual thinking journey:

• What medium will you use to visualize your thoughts? Medium here refers to the point of view and perspective of visualizing your startup. Are you going to do this from the perspective of the buyer of your product or you are going to do this from your perspective as the startup founder, which would include your startup goals, vision and objectives and the gradual steps at achieving them. Materials which instantly become useful in visual thinking include but not limited to Sketchbook, iPad, Copy paper, Table cloth or a Butcher paper. Any of these items would be good for a good sketch. You also have to place in mind that, it should be something that you can always refer to in the near future so as to keep track of your progress.

• Draw images by using single lines, connecting each to create images. It is essential to use single lines in drawing out your images to make it easier to identify and differentiate points from each other and to stress on understanding what impact you are creating with your drawing when viewed by a different person either on your team or somewhere else.

- Let your hand and fingers take the lead as you visualize. You really have to let your hand and fingers convert all the thoughts in your mind in way that would make the experience worth undertaking. And also important not to lose focus on what you are doing as that would confuse you along the way.

- Consider where you are going to place images on the page. By this, we are referring to the fact that you make use of arrows and directions to represent your growth from one place to

the other and to also make your destination clear. Insert directional arrows or points for the purpose of onward movement in achieving your various goals. You would not stay at one

place forever. Endeavour to work toward creating a visual journal of your startup ideas. You may also practice drawing sample images on a separate page even before starting out the original drawing.

Working with your brain's natural ability to organize information means that you really need to focus on letting go of the childhood programming that has stifled your creative talents and instead embrace your ability to draw, no matter how you think it looks. Visual thinking will enable you to take hold of a key that has the potential to unlock and open the door to achieve a whole new level of performance and design a better startup. Becoming a Visual Thinker only takes a little practice, persistence and commitment.

Some of the most famous thinkers in history, Albert

Einstein, Winston Churchill, and John F. Kennedy, have been visual thinkers. Leonardo da Vinci, considered by many to be the greatest thinker of all time, started every meaningful brainstorm with a visual. You can create what you want in your life. Visual thinking will help you get to where you want to go even faster.

We will tackle the remaining aspect of the BUSINESS MODEL DESIGN™ which we started previously. The two things we talked about included Value Proposition and Customer Development. We will narrow our discussion to one of the most important aspect of every startup business- Profitability and Revenue Development.

Revenue, Expenses and Resources
Step 3: Revenue Developments. As a Startup, what is most essential to you is profitability. As you create more repeatable revenue you can get yourself in a profitable state. Your immediate focus should be about revenue generation. Do you have more than one revenue stream? Understanding how to price your product or service also becomes important. Most often we find startup founders or owners pricing their products or service by mere guess work or by a gut feeling that their products will sell better at a certain price. What we often fail to consider is the fact that we are dealing with customers or people who desperately need our product or service offering so as to overcome petty challenges or problems they might be facing. The best thing to do is to therefore take feedback from customers concerning how much they would be willing to pay for your service. Another way to do this is to take the market average price of your product, without forgetting to inculcate your Unique Selling Proposition especially when you got competitors for your product or service offering.

The next thing to consider after your profitability is to keep track of your expenses. As a startup, what kind of expenses are you making? We hear all the time things like: "I have no expenses"; "I am not taking a salary". But you still need to understand that you are still an expense. Once you are starting a company, even though you do not take a salary, you need to understand that you are an expense. Your phone is an expense, your travel, fuel costs are expenses. Anything associated with your business is an expense. Understanding what those expenses are is critical as you grow more and more revenue. Once you identify these expenses, it is very necessary to trim them down as quickly as possible

Identify ways of bootstrapping your business. Bootstrapping refers to the technique of starting a business with existing resources to create something more valuable for costumers. It is very essential to identify idle resources around which you can use to boost more production and market value. At certain points in running your business it may be of essence to give out part of your company's equity to someone in exchange for investments, or grants to inject into the business. We will delve more into investments and equity sharing for startups another time.

Promotion, Team, Sales, and Funding
Step 4: Developing your team. Every thriving business succeeds on a team. Team management is one of the main challenges that most startup founders face. What kind of expertise do you need for your startup? The basic team members for any startup are the ideator, the promoter and the financial manager.

Step 5: Sales. Develop very good sales techniques that would see your product selling at either a faster rate or bringing in more revenue within the shortest possible time. Sales techniques to a larger extent depend on the type of product you are offering to customers. Some products are good to sell on the market whereas others could be sold personally to the consumers. No matter what, it is essential to determine which method would quickly generate more sales for you. By consulting for companies in Ghana and abroad this is one of the pitfalls I notice in most of them. Your business would succeed on a good sales strategy! Do not just put out your product and expect people to automatically buy them! It does not work that way. You as the sales manager or startup founder need to put in much work to sell as many products as possible so as to increase revenues for your business which is highly essential to sustain your business.

Final Step: Get to Work! After all the paper work, visual thinking, drawings, and all imaginary procedures are done, you really have to get to work to bring those plans into action. You have to start seeing the outcome of your work. Do not just sit aside and expect things to work out! A little word of advice: "Stop talking and Start Doing". Start testing your assumptions on the market by offering samples of your product and service to people for them to give you feedback on what is necessary or things to change about your product, design, etc. Look out for new ways of designing your product or service offering and implement them in your business model.

SUMMARY:
a) Visualisation is a tool which helps to plan effectively towards personal and professional achievements.
b) Business Model Design is a visual technique that can be used to simplify the entrepreneurial journey.
c) The Model includes Value proposition, Customer developments, Revenue developments, developing the team, Sales and the final step which is Implementation of what has been visualized.

20 IMPACT STORIES

"A life is not important except in the impact it has on other lives."- Jackie Robinson

Through my tough but fulfilling journey, by grace, my hardwork has impacted a number of talented people, some of whom are Henry Damulira and Braveheart Segbefia. Be inspired by their stories below:

Henry Damulira, born in Uganda now an innovator and entrepreneur. He faced many challenges, like many entrepreneurs from around the world. He came from a poor family, and as he grew up, he realized that he had a solution to a problem that many in his situation were facing. As a young child, he would fetch water by hand with the goal of saving enough money to buy a bicycle, which would allow him to fetch more water and make more money. So he made a wooden small box to keep in his savings. Like many people, Henry had trouble saving money in the wooden box because every time he could break the box and spend all the money before reaching his saving objective. Like one day he broke the wooden box and bought a baseball cap with the money he was saving for a bicycle.

In Africa roughly 90% of the population are unbanked, many of which lose their money, not from the ability to save, but because of having to keep all their money in their houses, leaving it vulnerable to theft, fire and over spending it before reaching their saving goal leading to poverty.

Seeing all of the issues the unbanked faced, Henry decided to start Fintech company called Airsave. His company innovated a Saving platform called a digital saving wallet that allows community members using mobile phone to create digital saving wallets and save a set amount of money for a given period of time using a mobile phone to enhance saving with no need to walk to a bank Hall. His innovation is now used by a financial institution called Airsave Sacco to serve the unbanked. Website: www.airsaveuganda.com. He started offline at his local church, allowing members to drop off money or valuables for a set amount of time. After seeing the success, Henry took his innovation digital. He introduced his innovation to a financial institution that took it and in only 2 weeks 3000 people across Uganda had signed on his platform saving money in their saving wallets created on their mobile phones.

After competing in the Uganda StartUp Cup competition where he came 1st, and taking 2nd place at the Africa StartUp Cup in Ghana where he met Emmanuel E. K. Nyame, now his mentor. Henry also represented Uganda in the world startup cup in Washington DC where he came 4th place in the world. Henry received an unprecedented amount of recognition from his country including being interviewed on the National Uganda Television Station and other media houses. He hopes to continue the success and grow Airsave beyond Uganda in the next few years.

Henry started nonprofit profit foundation called Airsave Development foundation, website: www.airsavefoundation.org focusing on financial inclusion and financial literacy in communities across Africa to empower youth and women.

Henry Damulira
President
Airsave foundation
+256702982218
www.airsavefoundation.org

BraveHeart Segbefia; the man who makes a fortune selling adventure in the wild.

A year ago, BraveHearts Expeditions was worth, 25,000 dollars. Today, it is worth several hundreds of thousands of dollars.

As I entered the *Hub Accra* that fateful morning, I was eager to meet a mentor who could help me on my journey to starting my own online company. About three months prior, I had conceived of what I believed to be a great idea, something that will completely cause a revolution in customer service delivery in Ghana, using the Internet, especially for blue-collar jobs. And I was determined to start see it propel me into billionaire status in a few months, or so I hoped.

So entering this mentoring session organized for young entrepreneurs who had been short listed for the American Embassy's Start Up Cup Competition, I was looking out for a mentor who would understand my doubts and constrains as a young Ghanaian man looking to start a business. Scouting around the small conference room, there were about four small groups, each comprising 5 entrepreneurs assigned to a mentor. But I realized something different about a particular group- the high level of energy and interaction between the entrepreneurs in the group and their mentor,who I must say was awkwardly dressed in a military-ish looking attire with thick jungle boots. Who is this guy, and why does he have these his entrepreneurs eating off of the palms of his hand. I wondered exactly what he was telling these young entrepreneurs and why they were all very attentive, laughing at his jokes, and energetically responding to what he was saying. No other mentor in the room had that kind of effect that he was having on his group.

I realized, upon joining his group, that not only did **Dziedzorm Segbefia** win the previous edition of the *Start Up Cup Competition*, he understood exactly where the young entrepreneurs found themselves, and on the whole, he understood the challenges young Ghanaian entrepreneurs and Start Ups face, and how easy it is to want to give up because he has been there. And for his group of mentees, they found in him the perfect mentor who walked where they are currently walking and actually defeated higher odds to achieve the success they hoped for. He perfectly understood them because he faced a higher challenge with his business idea. He inspires them because he defeated those odds.

Jay Jay as he is affectionately called is the Chief Expeditions Leader of an expeditions company founded not more than five years ago called **BraveHearts Expeditions**. *Wildlife and Adventures in Ghana? Is this guy crazy? Does he think we are in America?* That was what I thought about his business.

First of all, it is a luxury service, operating in a country having serious challenges recovering from a serious economic crisis. Necessities have become a lot more difficult to afford, talk less of someone paying for an adventure hiking trip through the Kwahu Forests, or climbing the Afajato, or Abseiling the Shai Hills. But the tenacity of Jay Jay has propelled what used to be a hobby into a full-fledged business in Ghana- a business worth several hundreds of thousands of Ghana Cedis, which gives its customers an experience of a life time in the African Jungles, and the highest peaks of the world.

How it all started
Jay Jay's first exposure to expeditions and the adventures of nature and wild life was through the **Head of States Awards Scheme**; an adventurous expedition program for Senior High Schools. Jay Jay was one of the key members

of his **Accra Academy HOSA Club,** who not only excelled in the Bronze, Silver and Gold expeditions, but went on to be one of the gold medalists in the country.

After school, he took this love for expeditions further to the international level where he assisted on a few expeditions in Africa especially to **Kilimanjaro**, where he rose through the ranks to leading his own expeditions 7 times to Kilamanjaro and **Mount McKinley** in the **U.S-** two of the seven highest peaks on earth. Just like many Ghanaian youth, it hasn't always been Jay Jay's idea to run his own business, especially not an enigmatic one like **BraveHearts Expedition**. He describes his venture into business as a matter of necessity and survival.

After SHS, he enrolled at the **Ghana Institute of Journalism**, then went to the Kwame Nkrumah University of Science and Technology to read law. Halfway through his law degree he lost interest in the course, and decided to study a Masters in Communications at the University of Ghana, instead. After that, he got a job, and was happy earning a salary, until tragedy struck- *well looking back today, he won't say it was a tragedy*- but he lost his job, he was fired! From then on, in his own words, it became a matter of survival. After unsuccessful attempts at getting a new job, the founder of BraveHearts Expeditions decided to use his greatest skill- expeditions, to provide his next meal. So he devised an expeditions program for Senior High School and University students to some of the common attraction sites in the country, **Boti Falls**, **Afajato Mountain** amongst others.

Then came the appetite to scale up to bigger expeditions, bigger clients, and bigger profits. But there was the challenge of finance. Almost every financial investor Jay Jay talked to, thought he was smoking something, to think that such a business idea would work in Ghana. He failed massively at raising the needed capital to make it work

"That's when I understood that business especially, if you find yourself where I was at that time; well-educated but jobless and broke, all that makes sense is where to get your next meal. For me I was no longer concerned about business plans, and pitching, all I cared about was where to get my next customer in order to afford my next meal." So when all the drive for investment did not work, he just switched into survival mode, looking for the next customer and the next, and the next. Scavenging from Senior High Schools, Universities, corporate entities (with little luck), to multi nationals, embassies and international organisations. That was when it all started to work. BraveaHearts Expeditions realized that their best clients would be entities of diasporan backgrounds and expatriate employees who wanted to experience the Ghanaian Wild for themselves, first-hand. From then on, Jay Jay and his BraveHeart Expeditions were in business. There was a stable flow of clients and sturdy flow of income.

Dealing with Business Pitches and Acquiring Grants.
Running expeditions is a capital intensive endeavour. One requires sleeping tents, protective gear, hi-tech security arrangements, trucks, and high-level expert training for staff, which cost over several thousands of dollars per staff. Braveheats needed some extra funding of some sort to survive. This time they opted for business competitions with the ultimate aim of getting grants to further scale up the business. So Jay Jay and his team enrolled in the 2013 edition of Enactus Business plan competition as well as the Start UP Cup 2013. They won both. They went on to the World Start Up Cup Competition and placed second. This earned Jay Jay **President Barack Obama's Washington Mandela Fellowship**, and a **10,000 dollar grant** for Braveherts. All these owed to Jay Jays unparalleled ability to sell his business in a pitch. He is one

of the best business pitchers in the country with his ability to persuade almost every judge that his expeditions Idea in Ghana makes sense and is extremely commercially viable. And he almost always succeeds. No wonder the **2014 Start Up Cup** contestants were eating out of his palms, listening to him with such avid attention. He knew and had the secrets to succeeding, not only in a business pitching contest, but making the impossible in business, possible.

BraveHeart Expedition's Success today. A year ago, BraveHearts Expeditions was worth, **25,000 dollars**. Today, it is worth **several hundreds of thousands of dollars.** With over **20 expeditions Sites in Ghana,** and **150 across Africa,** they have ran **6000 different expeditions in Ghana** alone since **2010.** BraveHearts Expeditions are able to take clients on one expedition from West Africa to Southen Africa, hiking, climbing mountains, abseiling amongst other adventurous activities.

The next time you hit an obstacle in life, stop and remember the BraveHeart Jay Jay Segbefia who says nothing is impossible!

An article written by Emmanuel Quist, Reporter- Pulse (www.pulse.com.gh)

The power of small beginnings; the story of Emi-Beth Quantson of Kawa Moka.

" We started so small. We were doing like just one cup of coffee a day and total sales of 100 cedis, fifty percent of which was family and friends."- Emi-Beth Quantson

"Think Big, Start Small, Act Now"- Steve Jobs
What will push a high-powered Chartered Accountant working for a prestigious international auditing firm like Price-WaterhouseCoopers to quit her job to start a coffee shop, selling one cup of coffee a day, some plates of food for as little as 100 cedis sales a day.

"We started so small. We were selling on average a cup of coffee a day with total sales of 100 cedis, fifty percent of which was to family and friends", Emi-Beth recounts. Starting small in business may just be the most practical way to get a business idea off the ground, especially in the face of inadequate supply of capital for startups. Unfortunately, not only are people impatient to start small, it doesn't feel like the true representation of the big dreams they have for their businesses.

Emi-Beth Aku Quantson is one of the few entrepreneurs setting a good example for Ghanaian entrepreneurs on the power of starting small, acting now and thinking big. She started the business that would later become Kawa Moka, as her final year entrepreneurship project in the Ashesi University. *"Starting the business was very random, actually. There was a gazebo in a beautiful garden in the then Labore campus of Ashesi. I saw a great opportunity to turn it into a nice place on campus where the population could come in for cool refreshments, snooker, and generally a nice place to chill out."* That space became the Lounge, Kawa Moka's forbearer. However, Ashesi would move to their ultra-modern campus in Berekuso and Emi-Beth could not run the Lounge for much longer, so she put her Accounting and Finance degrees to work. "There was a nice place I used to go for Coffee when I was working for PricewaterHouseCoopers in Kenya. The coffee was great, the business was inspiring, and the environment soothing. That reminded me of the Lounge and my dream for Kawa Moka." Ordinarily, Emi-Beth needed an ultra-modern coffee machine worth about GHC30,000, a space in Accra's most prime locations, the best décor and the biggest marketing budgets befitting of the size of her idea and the impact she wanted to make."My fellowship with the Tony Elumelu Entrepreneurship Program Award, helped me a lot. The program challenged me to start my business with the little I had. It may never happen if you wait for all the resources you need to start. A lot of the time we focus on what we don't have and forget the things we do have, like passion to see the business grow." Instead of waiting for the $150,000 she needed, Emi-Beth took an opportunity presented by the Hub Accra, now the beautiful Impact Hub in Osu Ako-Adjei, who had approached her to be their Chief Financial Officer.

" Before that, I shared my dream to start Kawa Moka with them, and they volunteered to make me start at the hub. Customers at the Hub are going to need food and coffee anyway, the space was beautiful, there were already tables and chairs, and it was located in a prime location in Accra. That was a perfect opportunity."

Kawa Moka has been growing at high speed since. They have moved from a small coffee maker to a relatively bigger one, diversified their products from coffee to some of the best fruit cocktails I have tasted. The business has moved from a capitalist venture to a social enterprise providing employment to socio-economically disadvantaged women including young girls transitioning from Senior High School to tertiary education.

Emi-Beth has won a couple of entrepreneurship awards including Startup Cup Ghana, not because of the size of her business but her entrepreneurial spirit and the potential of representing where Ghanaian entrepreneurship should be headed.

"The future is bright for Kawa Moka, we are looking to expand to other locations. We are also looking to train our women to be managers of these locations. This will ensure that their lot improve just as the business improves."

To young entrepreneurs, Emi-Beth's advice is not to wait for a million dollars before they start their business. You must endeavour to start with as little as you have, but dream and think big. With the right scale-up strategies you will be as big as you dreamt from the beginning.
" Truth is, if you are given one million dollars from the beginning, you will blow it in no time. Think big, start small and act now! That is the secret."

An article written by Emmanuel Quist, Reporter- Pulse (www.pulse.com.gh)

> "TO SUCCEED IT IS NECESSARY TO ACCEPT THE WORLD AS IT IS AND RISE ABOVE IT."- MICHAEL KORDA

21 REFERENCES

Algert, N. E & Watson K. (2002). Understanding conflict and conflict management.

Anaman Pauline& Armah Ernest. (2015 ,September 30) Sex Gender and corruption in Ghana.

Branson, R. (2012). Like a virgin: Secrets they won't teach you at business school. Virgin.

Econet Wireless Library. (Notes) Zimbabwe.

Frost, Robert (1916). The road not taken.

Jackson Chris& Wiens Jason(2015, September 13). The importance of young firms for economic growth. From Kauffman.org

Kaplan Robert(1999). The balanced scorecard. 45.

Kauffman Foundation Research Series: Firm Formation& Economic growth paper. (2010, July). The importance of Start- Ups in job creation & job destruction.

Macmillan Dictionary

Quist Emmanuel (2015,October 13). Meet the Boss: Braveheart Segbefia; the man who makes a fortune selling adventure in the wild. From www.pulse.com.gh
https://www.pulse.com.gh/news/business/meet-the-boss-braveheart-segbefia-the-man-who-makes-a-fortune-

selling-adventure-in-the-wild-id4205891.html

Yunus Muhammad (1999). Banker to the poor. 27. Bangladesh

Quist Emmanuel (2017, February 15). The power of small beginnings; the story of Emi-Beth Quantson of Kawa Moka. From https://www.pulse.com.gh/bi/strategy/coffee-love-the-power-of-small-beginnings-the-story-of-emi-beth-quantson-of-kawa-moka-id5055722.html

ABOUT THE AUTHOR

Emmanuel Nyame is a social entrepreneur and advocate with over a decade-long professional experience in private sector development, business development, access to financial and equity investment, economic and development issues, for diverse categories of micro, small and medium scale enterprises, non-governmental organisations, venture capitalists, governments, among a range of entrepreneurship development organisations.

His involvement with US Department of States' StartUp Cup, an accelerator program for startups, which he passionately launched while studying Economics and Mathematics at the university, brought renewed hope to young entrepreneurs in Ghana, Africa and propelled him to unimaginable heights among the startup ecosystem.

He is currently involved with Educational Communities Worldwide, a non-profit on a mission to bridge the skills gaps among students - a bold step towards addressing unemployment in his country. He also Co-founded SocialGood Ghana, as a member of United Nations Foundation's +SocialGood Connectors and Advisors community. He is constantly involved in activities geared towards helping achieve the Sustainable Development Goals.

He is on SXSW's advisory team for the annual accelerator program. He also serves as a First Democracy VC Partner of Indiegogo and MicroVenture's new equity crowdfunding platform.

Your Free Gift

Hi there!

It is such a great pleasure to connect with you today. As a token of appreciation, I would like to give you a free gift which includes thirty minutes free interaction to help you discover yourself, or to help refine your business ideas. Why not get in touch? Schedule a free appointment via email and do not forget to follow my rise above journey on social media via hashtag #RiseAboveTips.

Instagram - ek_nyame

Facebook - Emmanuel Nyame

Twitter - @eknyame

LinkedIn - www.linkedin.com/in/EmmanuelNyame

Primary Email - eknyame@gmail.com

I look forward to hearing your great stories. Let's rise above together!

Emmanuel!

www.ingramcontent.com/pod-product-compliance
Lightning Source LLC
Chambersburg PA
CBHW031420210526
45464CB00005B/1968